Casablanca
Tehran-Karaj
Urumqi
Hefei
Hyderabad
Ho Chi Minh City
Addis Ababa
Lima
Gauteng

AF478997

CAPACITY DEVELOPMENT

Approaches for Future Megacities

Bernd Mahrin (Editor)

Book Series
Future Megacities
Vol. 3

SPONSORED BY THE

Federal Ministry
of Education
and Research

The Book Series "Research for the Sustainable Development of Megacities of Tomorrow" is sponsored by the German Federal Ministry of Education and Research (BMBF) through the funding priority "Research for the Sustainable Development of Megacities of Tomorrow". The authors would like to thank the Ministry for this initiative, for the financial support, and for the extraordinary opportunity to connect activity- and demand-oriented research with practical implementation in various pilot projects targeting the challenges of Future Megacities.

The book series "Future Megacities" is published by Elke-Pahl-Weber, Bernd Kochendörfer, Lukas Born, Jan Müller and Ulrike Assmann, Technische Universität Berlin. The series contains the cross-cutting results of the nine projects. These results are the intellectual property of the authors.

Volume 3 "Capacity Development" of the book series is edited by Bernd Mahrin, Technische Universität Berlin (Department of Vocational Training).

Elke Pahl-Weber, Bernd Kochendörfer, Lukas Born, Carsten Zehner

The Book Series "Future Megacities"

The Global Urban Future

The development of future megacities describes a new quality of urban growth, as the pace and the dynamics of urbanisation today are historically unprecedented. At the beginning of the twentieth century, only 20% of the world's population lived in cities. Since 2010, however, the share of urban-dwellers has risen dramatically to above 50%. By 2050, the world population is predicted to have increased from 7.0 billion to 9.3 billion, and, by that time, 70% of people will be living in urban areas, many of them in urban corridors, city- or mega-urban regions [UN-DESA 2012; UN-Habitat 2012].

Urban areas contribute disproportionately to national productivity and to national GDP. Globally they concentrate 80% of economic output [UN-Habitat 2012; UNEP 2011]. Due to this, urban areas are also very relevant in terms of energy consumption. Although cities cover only a small percentage of the earth's surface[1], they are responsible for around 60–80% of global energy consumption as well as for approximately 75% of global greenhouse gas emissions [UNEP, 2011]. In the future, this will increasingly count for cities in so-called developing countries as they will be responsible for about 80% of the increases in the global annual energy consumption between 2006 and 2030 [UN-Habitat 2011]. Hence, cities are significantly contributing to climate change while, at the same time being the locations that have to deal with its devastating consequences, as many of them are located along the coast, close to rising sea levels, or in arid areas. Therefore, cities must take action to increase energy and resource efficiency, as well as climate-change mitigation and adaptation.

Megacities as a spreading phenomenon do have a special role in this context and illustrate the urban challenges of the future. These urban centres are not only reaching new levels in terms of size, but are also confronted with new dimensions of complexity. Hence, they are facing multifaceted problems directly affecting the quality of life of their inhabitants. In many cases, indispensable assets, such as social and technical infrastructure, delivery of basic services, or access to affordable housing are lacking. Capacities for urban management and legal frameworks tend to be chronically weak and are often insufficient when dealing with rapid population and spatial growth. Moreover, excessive consumption of resources such as energy or water is further aggravating existing problems.

In many countries, medium-sized cities, especially, are experiencing extraordinary growth rates. These „Future Megacities" are to be taken into consideration for sustainable urban development strategies, as they still offer the opportunity for precautionary action and targeted urban development towards sustainability [UNEP 2011].

BMBF's Funding Priority on Future Megacities

With its funding priority "Research for the Sustainable Development of Megacities of Tomorrow" the German Federal Ministry of Education and Research (BMBF) is focusing on climate-responsive and energy-efficient structures in large and fast-growing cities or megacities. The programme is a globally focused component of the Federal Government's High-Tech Strategy in the field of action on "Climate and Energy". Moreover, it is a part of the framework programme "Research for Sustainable Development" (FONA) of the BMBF.

In its main phase (2008–2013), the funding priority currently covers nine international projects in future megacities of Asia (Tehran-Region, Hyderabad, Urumqi, Hefei, Ho Chi Minh City), Africa (Casablanca, Addis Ababa, Gauteng), and Latin America (Lima). Each project focuses on a particular city working on a locally relevant thematic issue within the broader context of energy efficiency and climate change (for more details, see "Projects in Brief", p. 183 ff.).

An outstanding characteristic of the programme is the integration of the sustainable development concept. Ecological, economic, and social facets of the development of climate-responsive and energy-efficient structures in urban growth centres are considered in a comprehensive and long-term manner. In this context, the programme follows an innovative methodology ranging from analysing spatial, social, and technical dimensions in combination with applied research, to using broad methodological approaches such as pilot projects, action research, and research by design. Hence, the research approach here differs from other forms of fundamental research due to its practice-oriented focus that takes into account local needs as a basis for the development of applicable solutions. Therefore, the transdisciplinary research is conducted by interdisciplinary consortia with partners from research institutions, civil society, politics, and administration, as well as the private sector. International collaboration between project partners from Germany and the partner countries is an essential aspect of the programme. The objective of the Future Megacities Programme is to create good-practice solutions for sustainable urban development. Therefore, the bilateral teams perform the following tasks:

1. research, plan, develop, and realise technical and non-technical innovations for the establishment of climate-responsive and energy-efficient structures in an exemplary way
2. enable the city, along with its decision-makers and inhabitants, to bring about increased performance and efficiency gains in energy production, distribution, and use
3. demonstrate that the resource consumption and greenhouse gas emissions by the high energy-consumption-sectors can be reduced in a sustainable way in the future [DLR-PT 2012]

Outcomes and Results

Outcomes of the projects have been generated in different thematic fields of action. Within these thematic areas, a great variety of good practices for building up climate-responsive and energy-efficient structures in urban growth centres has been generated, ranging from scientific knowledge, to analytical instruments and strategic models, all the way up to realised pilot-projects, innovative technologies, applied products, and locally implemented processes.

Within the area of "Planning, Space, and Design", solutions for increasing energy efficiency in architecture and urban design, tools for integrated urban planning, and efficient management instruments for climate-change mitigation and adaptation have been developed. In the field of action on "Energy and Sun", concepts for the urban use of renewable energies with particular focus on solar power have been elaborated for different sectors in order to decrease the use of fossil fuels and to diminish carbon-dioxide emissions and air pollution. The topic "Mobility and Transportation" comprises concepts for sustainable transportation through intelligent management approaches, innovative planning instruments, and systems for enhancing public transit. The area of action on "Urban Resources" focuses on generating new approaches for the sustainable management of waste, the careful use of scarce resources such as water and land, as well as efficient material cycles in the industrial sector. In the field of "Governance and Local Action", models for stakeholder involvement, new approaches to inclusive decision-making processes, as well as community participation and bottom-up engagement, have been developed. Outcomes within the area of "Capacity Development" include measures of vocational training practices and other forms of knowledge transfer.

This book series presents results generated within these thematic fields of action in terms of cutting-edge research as well as practical outcomes. This particular volume focuses on capacity development activities in eight cities of the research programme. It contains examples of vocational training practices and of theoretical instructions in almost all fields of actions, as well as concepts for education, awareness-raising by different media, and governance related knowledge transfer. Other outcomes focus on the empowerment and enabling of communities in urban neighbourhoods. The articles show differences and similarities in the challenges faced, as well as respective approaches and practical solutions. Answers are given on innovative aspects, applicability, transferability, or dissemination of the solutions in the framework of future megacities in general.

Additionally, all participating cities and projects are presented in the appendix, where the complexity of the research programme, the different approaches, and a short overview of the most important outcomes are shown.

Sources

DLR-PT – Deutsches Zentrum für Luft- und Raumfahrt e. V. – Projektträger im DLR (2012): Research Programme Main Phase: Energy- and Climate Efficient Structures in Urban Growth Centres. http://future-megacities.org/index.php?id=48&L=1, 15.02.2013

Seto, K. C./Güneralp, B./Hutyra, L.R. (2012): "Global forecasts of urban expansion to 2030 and direct impacts on biodiversity and carbon pools". In: Proceedings of the National Academy of Sciences of the United States of America. http://www.pnas.org/content/early/2012/09/11/1211658109.full.pdf+html?with-ds=yes, 07.03.2013

Soya, E. (2010): "Regional Urbanization and the Future of Megacities". In: Hall, P./Buijs, S./Tan, W./Tunas, D.: Megacities–Exploring A Sustainable Future. Rotterdam, p. 57–75

UN-DESA United Nations Department of Economic and Social Affairs/Population Division (2012): World Urbanization Prospects: The 2011 Revision. Highlights. http://esa.un.org/unup/pdf/WUP2011_Highlights.pdf, 15.02.2013

UNEP United Nations Environment Programme (2011): Cities Investing in energy and resource efficiency. http://www.unep.org/greeneconomy/Portals/88/documents/ger/GER_12_Cities.pdf, 15.02.2013

UN-Habitat (2011): Cities and Climate Change: Policy Directions. Global Report on Human Settlements 2011, Abridged Edition. http://www.unhabitat.org/downloads/docs/GRHS2011/GRHS.2011.Abridged.English.pdf, 15.02.2013

UN-Habitat (2012): State of the World's Cities Report 2012/2013: Prosperity of Cities. http://www.un.int/wcm/webdav/site/portal/shared/iseek/documents/2012/November/UNhabitat%20201213.pdf, 15.02.2013

Notes

1   The current coverage of urban land on the earth's surface is often referred to as '2%' [UNEP 2011]. The predicted increase of urban land is dramatic: by 2030 urban land coverage will increase by 1.2 million km^2, thereby tripling the global urban land areas compared to the year 2000. In other words: 65% of the urban land coverage on the planet by 2030 was, or will be, under construction between 2000-2030, 55% of that expansion arising from urbanisation will occur in India and China [Seto, 2012]. According to Soya, cities tend to "Grow well beyond their defined administrative limits, typically spawning a multitude of suburbs in expanding annular rings. The outer edges thus came to be defined as ... part of the Functional Urban Region (FUR)" [Soya 2010, p. 58].

Index

Capacity Development through Media and Counselling

Appendix

TEHRAN-KARAJ: Formwork and reinforcement need proper workmanship [Nadia Poor-Rahim]

INTRODUCTION

ISFAHAN: Traditional handicraft with copper ware [Bernd Mahrin]

Capacity Development Approaches– What to Expect from this Book

Within the overarching objectives of greenhouse gas reduction, energy-efficiency, and sustainability, each of the Megacities projects followed some particular thematic focuses against different social, economic, and political backgrounds. These respective key aspects were related to the specific regional problems, deficits, development and potential capacities. These include amongst others rapid urban growth, loss of farmland, food security, increasing water shortage, waste management, danger of flooding, disproportionate energy consumption, energy-efficient urban fabric, environmental assessment, transportation and mobility, material resource efficiency, etc. Some of these subjects are comprehensively addressed in other volumes of this book series. The chapter "Projects in Brief" at the end of this book gives a more detailed impression of the Megacities projects.

Regardless of the various important research and action topics, capacity development emerged as a very important cross-cutting issue during the course of the projects. Reaching the aspired high standards of sustainability and greenhouse gas reduction in all megacities projects, needs the involvement of people with competencies and awareness—either as engineers, planers, managers, workers, or as users. Particularly with respect to the fact that most of the projects followed an action research approach, this is not only evident but even essential. That encouraged us to compile a choice of good-practice examples and auspicious capacity development approaches in this book, which may inspire other colleagues to meet similar needs and requests by using the instruments and adapting the concepts. To achieve this, all of the contributions in this book include hints and incentives; they explain how to get involved, offer links to further information and proved results, and expose conducive and obstructive determining factors.

As the Megacities projects are connected to different branches and fields of action and actually set different focuses inside these spheres, the book reflects a wide thematic spectrum. The articles are assigned to three chapters. However, intersections could not be completely avoided. The first chapter deals with governance and structural issues of vocational training and decision-making, and with approaches to build up local capacities. The second chapter is the most extensive one. It gives attention to designing and processing practical and theoretical trainings and instructions. The third chapter introduces some good practice examples of supporting media, guidance, and accompanying measures.

The book in your hand has the character of a capacity development atlas. This explains why all contributions follow the same structure. They all start with basic information to the project's region, to the initial situation and to special aspects of the action's settings in order to encircle the starting position. This is followed by noteworthy details concerning objectives, target groups, and parties involved to define the action's orientation. Subsequently, the description subjects, issues, contents, methods, scenarios, organisational aspects, instruments and products describe the course of action. Afterwards, indications of costs, necessary efforts, resources, and other requirements give an impression of the action's needed framework. Finally, the experience with the approaches and measures, as well as the implementation, transfer, and dissemination activities are explicated to complete the information.

Each of the fifteen articles goes back to a unique project with a special regional background, special political, social, economic, and ecologic conditions. And each of them has a special research approach and offers adjusted proposals, strategies, and solutions. On the one hand, the book wants to make all these singularities visible. On the other hand, it wants to point out that there are so many similar problems concerning megacities and their surroundings all around the world. This offers manifold chances for transfer and dissemination of the generated results, instruments, and products to develop the urgently needed capacities and people's awareness. This transfer is in no way limited to the Megacities projects, but goes far beyond them. You are invited to take benefit from the authors' experiences and to take it as challenge and motivation for your own work.

Acknowledgements

This publication was made possible by the support, contribution, and enduring collaboration of many researchers and experts from Germany and from the Future Megacities Projects' partner countries. The main phase of the projects extended from 2008 to 2013. The projects were funded financially by the German Federal Ministry of Education and Research (BMBF) in the framework of the German government's High-Tech-Strategy. The authors and the editor would like to thank all those involved for this support, which enabled the undertaking of the research work.

I would like to express my gratitude to the reviewers and experts of the Megacities Programme for their valuable comments, suggestions, and guiding questions expressed on several occasions, in conferences and seminars. My sincere thanks also goes to Dr. Andrea Koch-Kraft from the Project Management Agency of the German Aerospace Centre (DLR) for encouraging me to compile and to publish this capacity development atlas. Furthermore, I would like to cordially thank the members of the cross-project programme support from the Technische Universität Berlin (TUB) and from the TÜV Rheinland International Research Management, namely: Prof. Elke Pahl-Weber, Prof. Dr. Bernd Kochendörfer, Lukas Born, Carsten Zehner, Ulrike Assmann, and Thilo Petri. This team was responsible for the programme's scientific and practice-related profiling, as well as the public communication and comprehensive transfer activities. Without their personal engagement and professional support, the publishing of the "Future Megacities" book series would not have been possible.

Thanks are also due to the members of the Young Cities Project who were, without exception, open for the increasing impact of capacity development during the course of the project. I would also like to mention Prof. Dr. Johannes Meyser here, who was responsible for the capacity development dimension and to thank him for his support and advice concerning this book. Particular thanks also go to Cornelia Saalmann and to Mathias Orth-Heinz from the Young Cities Project Centre, who helped to overcome a series of obstacles due to the strict limitation of personnel and financial capacities, and who always had an open ear to the requests from the capacity development perspective.

A very special thanks is also owed to my Iranian friend and colleague, Masoud Rezaei-Badafshani, who supported the editing process with the accurate and reliable review and revision of the contributions. Finally, I would like to give my heartfelt thanks to the authors of this book, to the publishing company for their professional support, and to all of the many people involved in the relevant project activities in the partner countries and in Germany. On behalf of all of the contributors, I extend my sincere gratitude to all of the institutions and the people who will continue the projects' work in the field of capacity development. You are invited to use, and to adapt the results, products, and experiences, which are outlined in this book.

Bernd Mahrin
Berlin, March 2014

LIMA: Ceremony at a district's town hall in San Martín de Porres [Lukas Born]

HOW TO CHANGE STRUCTURES: GOVERNANCE-RELATED CAPACITY DEVELOPMENT

LIMA: Town Hall [Lukas Born]

Bibhu Prasad Nayak, Veena Aggarwal, Christine Werthmann, Magdalena Gack

The LPG Project: Collective Action for Fuel Transition among the Urban Poor

Keywords

Self-help Groups (SHG)
Cooperation
Collective Action
Trust
Liquefied Petroleum Gas (LPG)
Reduction of Deforestation
Slums
Social Capital
Energy Access for the Poor

Basic Information[1]

Location: India, Andhra Pradesh (AP), Emerging Megacity of Hyderabad
Ecology: Climate change is predicted to lead to extreme weather events, disastrous floods, heat waves, extreme droughts, and increasing water scarcity.
Population: (Hyderabad Metropolitan) 7,749,334, Population growth (decadal): India -17.64%; AP: 11.1% [Census of India 2011]. "Greater Hyderabad", a fast-growing metropolitan region in Southern India, will reach 10.5 million inhabitants by 2015.
Economy/Living Standard: Approximately one-third of the population lives below the poverty line and continues to suffer from severe food and health problems. The emerging megacity experiences rapid economic growth enabling higher living standards and modern lifestyles for the emerging middle class. This is, however, accompanied by escalating energy and resource consumption and constantly increasing greenhouse gas emissions per capita.
Governance: The core modules of analysis in the project follow the hypothesis that "getting the institutions right" is one main key to solve the problems of sustainable resource use in general and sustainable demands on climate and energy in particular. Whether or not a society will be able to cope with the impact of climate change and increased scarcity of energy depends on its capacity to change human behaviour. This requires changing institutions, defined as "sets of rules" and governance structures, i.e., those "modes of organisation" that are necessary to put rules into practice.
Project Focus: The project's main subjects are climate and energy in a complex transition process towards sustainable mitigation and adaptation strategies by changing institutions, governance structures, lifestyles, and consumption patterns in Hyderabad. Given the natural,

social, and economic context of the emerging megacity, the question arises: what can be considered a reasonable response to the anticipated climate change impact? This is the guiding research question of the project. In order to try and answer this question, it was necessary to explore greenhouse gas mitigation and adaptation strategies and ways towards increased energy efficiency and renewable energy.

Initial Situation

Of the 2.7 billion people without access to clean cooking fuel in the world, 0.84 billion live in India. This constitutes 72% of India's total population, with 0.75 billion living in rural India and 0.9 billion living in urban and peri-urban regions [International Energy Agency 2011]. Over 33% of India's urban population is still using biomass-based cooking fuels. The use of biomass-based cooking fuels is predominant among the urban poor living in slums, and causes complex problems:

- Adverse impact of use of firewood as a cooking fuel on health and the (urban) environment due to smoke and the resultant morbidities.
- Poor and marginalised people suffer from the situation. It mainly affects women and children who spend the most time close to the cooking area. Poor families who live in smaller houses and do not have access to smokeless firewood stoves suffer from higher exposure to the smoke.
- An additional problem is the time-consuming collection process and related hardships. People from poor households either collect fuel wood from nearby shrubs, avenue plantations, or else they buy it from the open market. Those who collect the fuel wood locally spend about eight to ten hours per week for its collection and walk up to 10 km to fetch firewood.

Special Background in the Field of Culture

In order to obtain a Liquefied Petroleum Gas (LPG) connection, households must invest in a stove, the cylinder (security deposit for the cylinder and the cost of fuel), a regulator, and documentation charges. This often amounts to an average monthly income of a slum dweller and most often households cannot afford these initial payments. The study team found that there is no available government scheme under which the urban poor can pay for the connection in instalments. Neither does a government-financing scheme exist under which

they can avail a loan on soft terms. The "Deepam" scheme, a capital subsidy for availing gas connections in Andhra Pradesh, also has limited reach.

Objectives and Targets

A transition towards cleaner cooking fuels like LPG has the potential for improving the quality of the environment in urban areas, for a more efficient use of energy, as well as for contributing to the halting of deforestation. Thus, the project team decided to experiment with a community-based collective action approach for facilitating the shift from firewood to LPG for the urban poor.

The **objective** of the project is to facilitate transition towards cleaner cooking fuel among the urban poor through community-based resource mobilisation and sharing. The **rationale** behind this idea is to support a self-help solution for the poorest inhabitants in Hyderabad. Saving within a group is often easier, as the discipline for saving comes with social relationships between the participants and the promise of each member to contribute to the group. The project facilitates resource pooling to meet the initial, upfront costs and thereby enables poor households in urban slums to shift to cleaner and modern fuels, like LPG.

Target Groups

The group targeted with this approach was exclusively urban women who were still cooking with firewood and were, at the same time, not eligible for any support from a government scheme. The focus on women was obvious due to two important points. Firstly, it is mainly the women who cook and thus also suffer from the adverse impact of cooking with firewood. Secondly, self-help initiatives often work reasonably well within communities of women. The educational background of these women was not of great significance for the project implementation. However, the participants all belonged to low-income households living in urban slums in Hyderabad. The pilot project focused on facilitating the group formation and consensus-building among the women; additionally, the appropriate use of LPG was explained to the self-help group (SHG) members when required.

Parties Involved

The concept was developed by The Energy Resource Institute (TERI) and the Humboldt Universität zu Berlin. The implementation of the project was only possible with strong support from APMAS, a local NGO. APMAS has already been working with slum households in Hyderabad for many years and was thus familiar with the communities and their inherent problems, as well as conflict resolution mechanisms. Furthermore, the staff members of APMAS were trusted by the community members. This facilitated a successful project implementation.

Subjects, Issues, and Contents

Regarding the problems and difficulties of using traditional cooking fuels, the project team tried to use a community-based collective action approach for facilitating the shift from firewood to LPG for the urban poor. The project was developed by Humboldt Universität zu Berlin and TERI. With the support of a local NGO, women were empowered to implement the project themselves.

Methods, Scenarios, and Organisation

Before implementing the pilot project, a household survey was conducted in order to better understand energy-use patterns within the city. Moreover, a trust game gave information about trust patterns among urban households. Additionally, interviews have been conducted to increase the understanding of firewood/LPG uses. The pilot project commenced in March 2011 with two slums identified for the project. These were Banjara Colony and Nandanavanam in LB Nagar area in Hyderabad city.

Instruments, Products, and Learning

The pilot project has achieved its objective of enabling all sixty member-households to obtain an LPG connection and the required cooking accessories, thereby creating a direct impact to the participating households. All of the resources have been mobilised by the LPG group mem-

Fig. 6   Conducting interviews [Nayak]

Fig. 7   Conducting interviews [Werthmann]

Fig. 8   Discussion with slums' representatives [Nayak]

bers themselves without any financial support from the government or any outside agency. The role of the project team was limited to facilitating interaction with local gas agencies and building the capacity of the community to form LPG groups, encouraging the members to mobilise resources, organising regular meetings of the group members for conflict resolution, and improved relationships. Giving an incentive to community-based solutions, the approach enables the households to jointly face their material needs instead of being reliant on the state.

Costs, Efforts, Resources, and Preparation

Local gas dealers agreed to provide connections at INR 3,600 (1 INR equivalent to 0.02 USD) per single cylinder connection with LPG stove and other necessary accessories. Each group agreed on the resource pooling mechanisms and decided to mobilise a certain amount of money each month. With these resources, every month, a few member households were able to receive an LPG connection. Those households in both groups were selected by a lottery.

All of the resources were mobilised by the group members themselves. The costs involved are minimal when compared with the outcomes of the project. The actual project costs remained well within the planned costs of this low-cost project. The cost of coordination and capacity building has huge economies of scale. Hence, the cost-effectiveness can be enhanced when other such groups are covered within a specific slum and more slums are involved within a specific area in the city. The costs would have been lower if the two groups had been located in the same slum.

Essential Requirements

The realisation of the project depended on the willingness of all the member households of the saving groups to contribute to the build-up of trust in social cooperation. The realisation of a pilot project is easier in slums with active NGO involvement as a local partner. Moreover, the interaction with LPG distributors is crucial for the project success.

Experiences

The major difficulties anticipated with the upscaling of the pilot to other slums in Hyderabad is the lack of cooperation from the distribution agencies. A government directive to the agencies in recognising such groups and extending cooperation can help in upscaling the pilot project.

Upscaling of the pilot project is easily possible in slums with active NGO involvement as the catalyser to support the formation of self-help groups (SHG).

Implementation

The Government of India is working on a scheme to provide one-off financial assistance of INR 1,400 to households for taking up LPG connections [Economic Survey 2010–2011, Government of India, p. 269]. Our community-based, resource-pooling model can complement this proposed scheme, because the assistance of INR 1,400 (against the actual upfront cost of INR 3,600 to INR 4,200) will not enable many poor households to pay the remaining amount. Hence, institutionalising such collective action initiatives has the potential to expand energy access

for the poor. These collective action groups also have the potential to curb illegal connections, since the applications are scrutinised at the community level before coming to the LPG distributor. Involving local NGOs can be an essential driver for successful project implementation when they follow highly participatory approaches based on long-term commitment in the communities and the respective trustful relationship with the participants. The implementation of such approaches mainly requires facilitation capacities.

Transfer and Dissemination Activities

The success of the pilot project has resulted in enormous interest among other households in the slum to form such groups and to take advantage of the opportunity that LPG offers. This increased willingness of other households is influenced by the success of the LPG group in the slums. Such interest has also been observed in neighbouring slums by the field force of our NGO partner APMAS.

For more Information

General information about the LPG project can be found at the TERI homepage.

http://www.teriin.org/index.php?option=com_ongoing&task=about_project&pcode=2008UD06 or at the Sustainable Hyderabad Project Website

http://www.sustainable-hyderabad.de/implemation/pilot-project.html#PP4

In order to obtain materials and more information, please contact the authors via email.

References

Government of India (2011): *Energy, Infrastructure and Communications*. http://indiabudget.nic.in/budget2011-2012/es2010-11/echap-11.pdf, 02.12.2012

International Energy Agency (2011): *World Energy Outlook* 2011. IEA, Paris

Notes

1   Written by Srinivasa Srigiri, Humboldt Universität zu Berlin.

SOWETO
YOU'VE COME
A LONG WAY
NOW LET'S GO
EVEN FURTHER
METROPOLITAN
Together we can
LIFE | FUNERAL | EDUCATION | RETIREMENT | HEALTH | INVESTMENT

GAUTENG: Encouragement by the local government [Carsten Zehner]

Michael Knoll, Johannes Rupp

EnerKey Long-term Perspective Group (ELPG)—A Format to Introduce Long-term Thinking in Today's Decision-making

Keywords

Long-term Thinking
Shaping the Future
Interdisciplinary/transdisciplinary Approach
Vision/Mission
(Long-term) Objectives/Targets
Implementation Strategies

Basic Information

Location: Gauteng Province, Republic of South Africa (RSA), the smallest province in South Africa with just over 18,000 km² covering 1.4% of the total area of South Africa. High share of informal settlements in Gauteng: 19% of all households [StatsSA 2012b]

Population: Gauteng Province has a total of 12.3 million inhabitants or 3.9 million households. Gauteng's population corresponds to 23.7% of the total population of South Africa [StatsSA 2012a]. Major cities are: Johannesburg, Ekurhuleni, and Tshwane (Pretoria). Combined, they have a population of 8,958 million inhabitants and cover an area of 5,742 km². This indicates a relatively low density of 1,560 inhabitants per km² compared to a European city, like Berlin with 5,485 inhabitants per km². Gauteng is the fastest growing province, with an expected population of up to 20 million inhabitants by 2040 [Wehnert; Knoll; Rupp 2011].

Economy: Gauteng Province is the economic hub of South Africa; generating one-third of the country's GDP or 10% of the GDP of Africa as a whole. There is a high inequality: Gini-coefficient 0.57 for South Africa (Germany 0.3/China 0.41/USA 0.4)

Initial Situation

The energy sector in South Africa is characterised by a fragile security of supply (repeated blackouts), high emissions due to coal fired power production, massive energy inefficiencies in the industrial and commercial sector, insufficient access to electricity by the urban poor and, health and safety risks due to the use of obsolete and dangerous fuels by the poor. Several (inter)departmental and municipal policy papers circulate in Gauteng Province, formulating ambitious visions, objectives, and targets that address sustainable energy solutions and options for Gauteng as a low-carbon city region.

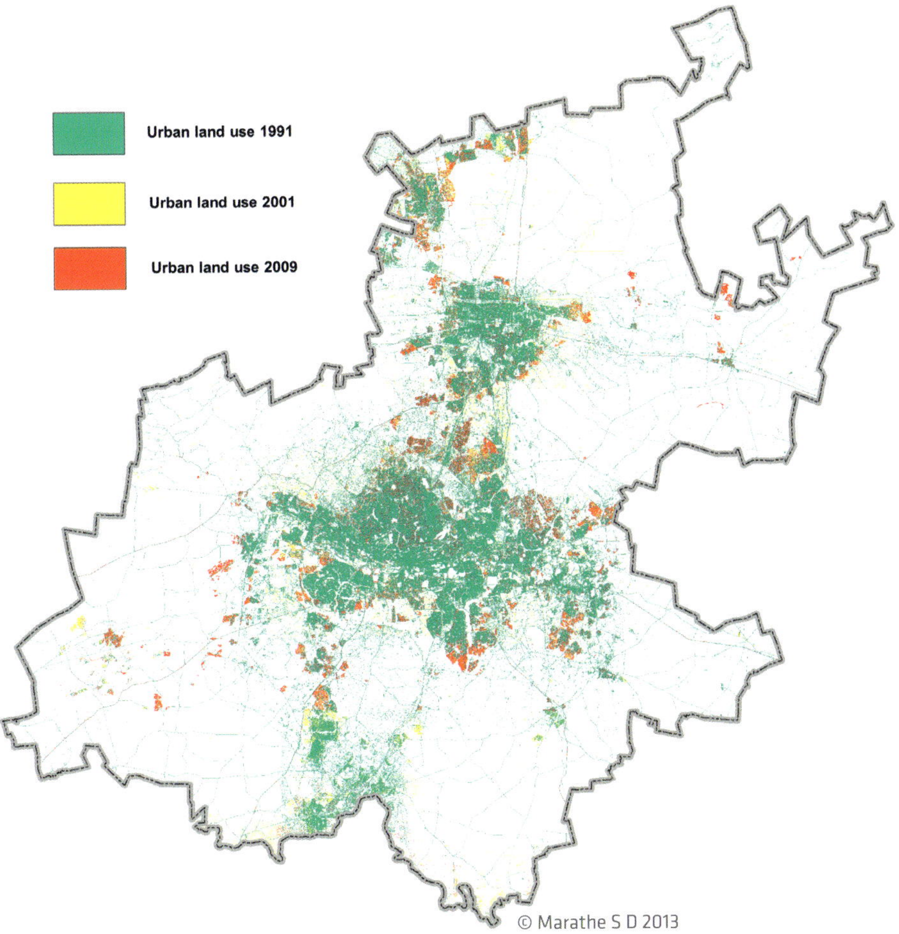

Against this background, the EnerKey project (Energy as a Key Element of an Integrated Climate Protection Concept for the City Region of Gauteng) aimed at developing integrated solutions for a sustainable energy future for the province of Gauteng. One major challenge was to integrate the fragmented knowledge within the province. Presently, the various stakeholders have quite different perspectives as to what key problems and possible solutions with respect to a low-carbon energy future might be. To integrate those different views, the EnerKey Long-term Perspective Group (ELPG) has been established. The ELPG provided a platform for experts and stakeholders with different professional and academic background to explore and discuss strategic options for energy and climate policies and actions under a long-term perspective.[1] A further function of the ELPG was to gather and assess information as part of the EnerKey research process and to disseminate preliminary EnerKey results to key stakeholders. Also, it enabled the incorporation of views and wishes of South African key stakeholders into the project in a participatory manner. Thus, it ensured that research questions were framed according to the local demand.

Fig. 2   Impressions from the Witsand iEEECO Housing-Project, a best-practice example for an integrated energy-efficient, low-income housing concept [IZT, 2011]

Legacy of Apartheid—Still a Meaningful Factor in South African Politics

Since 1994, numerous South African policies and different laws, ordinances, etc. have been approved, mainly to address issues to overcome the negative legacy of apartheid. These issues include, inter alia, social inclusion, poverty alleviation, improvement of living standards, and black empowerment. There have been important successes, but target dates, for example, for the eradication of backlogs in municipal services like "access to electricity" by 2013 and "housing" by 2014 will certainly not be achieved. Despite ongoing political rhetoric in the light of financial and institutional constraints, especially services for the poor are not delivered to the extent and in time as promised and required. One reason for this is that South African policies have thus far failed to generate an interconnected economic, social, and ecological development that allows the connection of sometimes opposing interests in terms of economic growth and distributive justice, global competitiveness and informal economy, use of domestic energy resource coal and "greening" the economy, increasing efficiency in all sectors, and job creation, etc.

Politicians and government administration are therefore under permanent pressure to close the gap between pledges made and unsatisfied demand with short-term actions, which often obscures the view for mid- to long-term effects of chosen approaches and decisions.

All three levels of government (national, provincial, and municipal) have been trying to accelerate the transformation process post-apartheid, particularly in terms of improving the appalling living conditions of the poor. Nevertheless, looking at the short-, medium- to long-term consequences of current government activities, a number of distinctive features are striking. Since 1994, for example, a great success is the number of completed dwellings in the Reconstruction and Development Programme (RDP). Nonetheless, houses are often of such poor quality that the need for medium-term renovation is already foreseeable. Although far-reaching goals are on the political agenda, ambitious policies exist, standards are defined, and sustainable interventions are known and, furthermore, "good practice" has already proven its feasibility, several factors—such as planning constraints, insufficient financial resources for implementation, and a lack of knowledge—hamper mass rollout of good practice. These kinds of proceedings satisfy today's needs for rapid service delivery, but simultaneously do not consider the mid- to long-term (positive or negative) effects of these activities. Therefore, a set of open-ended questions has to be answered, namely: Which steps are necessary to transfer good theoretical policies to the real world? Who should be the primary campaigner and take the lead? How can cooperation and collaboration of all relevant stakeholders be focused?

Objectives of the EnerKey Long-term Perspective Group

Within the EnerKey project, the ELPG was a format to explore strategic options with a long-term perspective. Its motto was: "Which decisions need to be taken today, in order to be consistent with long-term trends and requirements, as well as to contribute to sustainable development within a 20 to 30 years' time horizon." The focus is on implementation strategies ("How can successful sustainable approaches be applied on a large scale?") and on integrated strategies that go beyond sector specific perspectives.

The following major tasks and functions were considered by the ELPG:
- Identification of existing visions and ongoing processes (Gauteng, cities, sectors);
- Derivation and specification of research questions (priorities, linkage with other research fields);
- Development of implementation strategies (dissemination into institutions, recommendation for pilot actions, broad diffusion);
- Feed-in of regional expertise into the EnerKey research and implementation process.

Another major aim was to create ownership of the EnerKey research results among Gauteng's stakeholders. It is a prerequisite that outcomes of EnerKey will actually be sustained. Again, this is linked with activities to find scientific answers to frame and support implementation of the Gauteng Integrated Energy Strategy (GIES) and to develop needed competences and capacities there.

Target Groups of ELPG and their Position within the Energy System

Target groups of the ELPG were stakeholders from government, academia, private sector, and civil society , who agree to work on long-term perspectives based on current decision-making and implementation.

The aim was to address those people working on the decision-making level, acting as multipliers or intermediaries, as well as those involved in operational processes.

Institutions and Involved Persons in Carrying ELPG

Thus far, the ELPG has provided opportunities for discussion for more than 150 stakeholders who come from a wide variety of backgrounds and institutions, including:
- Provincial and municipal government: e.g., Gauteng Department of Local Government and Housing (GDLGH)/Economic Development/Infrastructure Development/Transport, etc.

Figs. 3 + 4 Impressions from discussions during ELGP meetings [IZT, 2008/2010]

- Academia: University of Johannesburg/University of Pretoria/CSIR—Council for Scientific and Industrial Research/Energy Research Centre, University of Cape Town
- Private sector: national energy utility Eskom, financial institutions (DBSA—Development Bank of Southern Africa), consultancies (SEA—Sustainable Energy Africa/Peer Africa Ltd., etc.
- Civil society
- Miscellaneous: GCRO—Gauteng City-Region Observatory, etc.

ELPG Approach—From Visions to Implementation

The ELPG approach follows a clear workflow and a sequence of topics, linking visionary long-term perspectives with concrete implementation strategies. In detail, the ELPG approach covers, firstly, basic research on energy related policies, stakeholder constellation, socio-economic development, trends, and sector-specific issues; secondly the scenario-building process, collaboratively undertaken; and, thirdly, the concentration on applied research that focuses on implementation strategies and defining concrete interventions and suitable frame conditions.

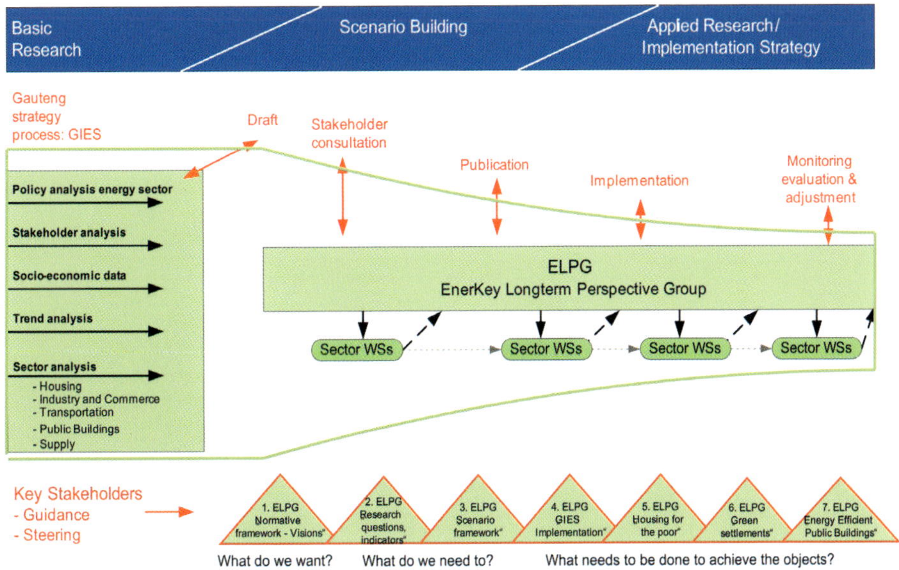

The activities of ELPG were closely aligned with the development and facilitation of the implementation of GIES as a major provincial strategy process.

Subjects and Contents of Work

The workflow of ELPG meetings has started with a broad scope, defining a normative framework and visions for Gauteng, with a time horizon of 2040. Based on this, overall research questions and indicators have been elaborated and discussed, before developing a scenario framework and identifying implementation challenges for GIES. The focus of recent ELPG meetings has been the facilitation of implementation activities as defined in GIES. They focused on concrete issues such as "Housing for the Poor", "Green Settlements", and "Energy Efficiency in Public Buildings". All of the ELPG meetings have taken place in conjunction with relevant South African and German project partners, and in close collaboration with sectorial workshops.

Structure and Working Environment

ELPG meetings took place twice a year as a one-day event. The meetings are scheduled with an input component with presentations from South African and German experts and a dialogue component with guided discussions, organised as working group sessions. The meetings are generally organised in an inspiring surrounding, with on-site visits—for instance, inspecting energy performance of public buildings or living conditions of low-income houses. This enables a special atmosphere for discussion in a situation that is separate from the routine of daily work.

Outcomes, Collaboration, New Initiatives

ELPG meetings are summarised in comprehensive minutes, which allow participants and project partners to get direction and support for their daily work on creating suitable conditions for integrated long-term planning. Thus, the minutes also help to find joint collaboration activities as possible follow-ups. Here, networking activities are supported by integrating the agenda and list of participants in the minutes.

A concrete activity out of the ELPG was a jointly developed normative socio-economic framework for energy scenarios for Gauteng 2040. They have been the basis for the modelling of different energy routes for Gauteng (by the TIMES-Model in Module 1). The different routes cover projections of desired developments in energy infrastructure, energy supply, energy services, and mitigation goals.

Another concrete activity has comprised the establishment of an interdepartmental "task force" to align and organise different joint activities between and within the provincial and local government—for example, the establishment of a Public Building Registry. More broadly, the ELPG has created an atmosphere of trust and ownership, which is expressed in open discussion and information sharing, as well as stable working relationship over the years. This message is coherent with statements from EnerKey partners given in the impact analysis [cf. Knoll/Rupp 2012].

Responsibilities, Task Sharing, and Adoption of Format

The ELPG was chaired by representatives of GDLGH in cooperation with the Institute for Future Studies and Technology Assessment (IZT) in Berlin, discussing the selection of topics and participants.

But the ELPG also pursued a strong participatory approach. The work programme was collaboratively defined by its members, focusing on core requirements of Gauteng Province. Furthermore, during the project, the coordination and invitation for the meetings has been handed over to an ever-greater extent from IZT to GDLGH and its Energy Office. The Energy Office was the first intervention of GIES and thus, task sharing created visibility and ownership for the Energy Office. In this process, IZT was responsible for organising scientific contributions and the facilitation of the meetings when they are held in South Africa. Meanwhile, several South African partners have adopted the format of the ELPG approach and organised their own workshops under the label of the ELPG, focusing on long-term perspectives.

Essential Requirements

The success of the ELPG in terms of transferring results and knowledge to the ground depends on a set of key factors, such as the correct composition of participants and a certain continuity of participation. The ideal participant of ELPG is a stakeholder who has the authority to make decisions and simultaneously is open-minded for long-term thinking and is willing to participate on a continuous basis. The latter however, has proved to be rather difficult. One reason is that in South Africa, government employees, in particular, frequently change positions (within government or in industry). Thus, during its five years of existence, the ELPG now consists of a small permanent core group and a fluctuating wider circle of participants. Another key success factor is the selection of relevant issues, which touch on-site challenges and help to find solutions. If local stakeholders do not see the added value of such an exercise, they will neither support the process, nor take ownership for its outcome. Therefore, ELPG pursues a participatory approach to meet on-site requirements and to set the agenda of the meetings.

Lessons Learnt

The format of the ELPG proved to be highly suitable to address its objectives, namely a collaborative agenda setting within the research project, the involvement of practitioners and decision-makers in this process, and a mutual exchange of knowledge and ideas. The high pressure for immediate implementation in a fast-growing megacity leaves little time for long-term planning. So one key challenge of the ELPG was to provide space for creativity and "out-of-the-box" future thinking, but simultaneously routing this creative process into both current and upcoming on-site requirements, in order to develop results with direct value-added for society. The participants of the ELPG were highly motivated to take up this challenge and actively use this opportunity for long-term strategic planning.

From the dynamics of the ELPG within the EnerKey project, some lessons that have been learnt can be drawn from now. We consider this to be relevant for the implementation of similar processes in other cities or fast-developing countries:

- High turnover of staff—especially in administration—undermines continuity of work. Thus, identifying key people and/or having commitment of institutions to collaborate continuously are crucial.
- This also applies to commitment of decision-makers from the public and the private sector. If they do not collaborate to an adequate extent, implementation is hampered.
- The perceived importance of energy and climate change issues for the development of the province and its people has increased in Gauteng over time. Embedding energy and climate change issues into ongoing and future activities supports the raising of awareness for comprehensive and sustainable solutions. This is also a primary reason for an enduring engagement of several stakeholders.
- Identifying common issues of interest and creating ownership among partners is central to sustaining structures and processes of bilateral applied research. However, another prerequisite for a fruitful collaboration is the availability of adequate resources—budget, time, capacity—for all partners. In this respect, the lack of adequate and targeted co-funding for the South African research partners has heavily limiting their engagement—and as a consequence has dampened the uptake of results developed within EnerKey.
- The involvement of administration and politicians grows with enhanced visibility of added value. However, a stronger political buy-in is still desirable.
- Stakeholder processes can be substantiated by defining and implementing pilots that have the potential for mass rollout.

Implementation in the Project's Context

The ELPG pursues a strong interdisciplinary and transdisciplinary approach, incorporating views and perspectives of various stakeholders within the project consortia—for example, by taking up sectorial work of project partners—and from the participants involved in ELPG meetings. Up to now, this has improved ties between people and institutions, such as government and academia. Furthermore, ELPG also promotes an integrated approach through the variety and complexity of topics that are being addressed, in particular by linking current decision-making with long-term perspectives.

Transfer and Dissemination Activities

Thus far, the ELPG format has received positive feedback. Several South African partners—such as the CSIR or Energy Office of GDLGH—have already applied this format for their own events, by using the label and incorporating its mission. Furthermore, similar formats have been initiated—such as the interdepartmental "task force"—to align and merge individual activities.

For more Information

Further information on the ELPG is accessible on the EnerKey website. All the meetings held by the ELPG are well documented on the EnerKey website, which provides the minutes of the meetings, including the agenda and list of participants, as well as presentations free of charge for download.

http://www.enerkey.info/index.php/Stakeholders-and-Socio-economic-Drivers/enerkey-long-term-perspective-group.html

References

Knoll, M./Rupp, J. (2012): *EnerKey Impact Assessment. Results of Online-Survey.* http://www.enerkey.info/images/stories/intern/module2/Documents/enerkey_m2_report%20online-survey_dec_2012.pdf, 08.10.2013

StatsSA (2012a): *Census 2011. Census in brief.* Report No. 03-01-41, Pretoria

StatsSA (2012b): *Census 2011. Provinces at a glance.* Report No. 03-01-43, Pretoria

Wehnert, T./Knoll, M./Rupp, J. (2011): *Socio-Economic Framework for 2010 set of EnerKey Energy Scenarios.* http://www.enerkey.info/images/stories/intern/module2/Documents/enerkey_m2_scenario_assumptions_2010_may_2011.pdf, 08.10.2013

Notes

1 The ELPG is located within the EnerKey project in Module 2 "Stakeholders and socio-economic drivers" and closely linked to Module 1 "Integrated Modelling".

HYDERABAD: Social survey in Vemulavada [Julian Sagebiel]

Julian Sagebiel, Christian Kimmich

Building Local Capacities to Improve the Quality of Electricity for Agriculture and to Enhance Energy Efficiency

Keywords

Farmer Training
Technical Intervention
Energy-irrigation Nexus
Rural-urban Linkages
Rural Development
Capacity Building

Basic Information

Location: The capacity development activities have taken place around the town of Vemulavada in Karimnagar District, Andhra Pradesh, India—150 km north of the emerging megacity of Hyderabad. Two particular villages, Sangula and Namiligundupally, were selected for the capacity development activities.

Climate: The area is slightly hilly and surrounded by forests. The river Mula Vagu runs through Vemulavada. Its use as a resource for irrigation however is limited, as the river is dry during most months of the year.

Population: The population of Vemulavada is around 60,000.

Economy: The majority of the rural population is involved in agricultural activities. The main crops are rice and cotton.

Resources: The principal source of irrigation is groundwater and electric pump sets are employed to draw the water.

Initial Situation

Most farmers in this area, as in many other regions in India, rely on groundwater irrigation extracted by electric pump sets. They suffer from ever-decreasing groundwater levels and low electricity quality. The existing policy—supplying electricity free of charge to the farmers—discourages the utilities from investing in the agricultural grid, while the farmers lack incentives to improve the energy efficiency of their pumps. As the problem was already detected a long time ago, several-demand side measures (DSM) were made compulsory by the government. However, these implementations failed in most cases. The reasons are manifold, but one

major fault was that top-down approaches were sought, whilst grass-roots interventions were neglected. An example: in 2004, the government implemented a regulation stating that farmers would only receive free electricity if they installed capacitors, frictionless foot valves, and other DSM. Although capacitors were given to the farmers free of cost, most farmers did not install the capacitor or removed it shortly after installation. The primary reason for this was that farmers faced problems due to a lack of knowledge on how to maintain the capacitors. Instead of improving power quality, the capacitors led to an increased number of burnouts and prevented motors from starting. Research conducted within the Sustainable Hyderabad project revealed that many farmers were unwilling to install capacitors because they felt that a capacitor would be harmful to the motor.

Special Background in the Field of Culture

A unique characteristic of the area is the governance of electricity supply. Electricity distribution is managed by a cooperative society, Cooperative Electricity Supply Society Sircilla Ltd (CESS), which is different from the usual distribution system of large state-owned companies. CESS is often mentioned as a best-practice example for undeveloped, largely agricultural regions.

A watershed programme—unrelated to the trainings described here—was initiated in 2003 in several villages near Vemulavada. Apart from increasing groundwater tables in the respective regions, the programme included manifold capacity-building and job creation measures.

Objectives and Targets

One objective of the pilot project was to demonstrate that DSM would be implementable if top-down and bottom-up approaches were combined. In particular, 900 capacitors have been installed in agricultural motors. As the negative experience with capacitors led to an initial aversion of farmers to technological advances, one major precondition of the project was to raise awareness and build local capacities of the affected farmers. It was anticipated that

Fig. 3   Motor rewinding in a local repair shop [Kimmich]

increased knowledge of the technology, in combination with guidelines on how to maintain the capacitor, as well as other equipment, would lead to a sustainable outcome. It was further hoped that, by forming farmers' groups, the relationship between CESS and the farmers improves, allowing a "win-win" situation to emerge.

Target Groups

The target groups are:
- Farmers who use electric motors for groundwater pumping: the educational background varies strongly. While some farmers are illiterate, others have as much as twelve years of schooling. There are also farmers who have a relatively strong technical background.
- Local electricians who install capacitors: they have a college degree, which qualifies them as electricians (ITI), however, their knowledge on theoretical and practical issues with motors is limited.

Parties Involved

The pilot project is led by the Division of Cooperative Sciences and the Division of Resource Economics at Humboldt-Universität zu Berlin. The lead partner selected a group of local partners according to the project requirements and in order to facilitate collaboration, ownership, and commitment among these partners. The following local partners were chosen:
- The implementing partner, a cooperatively governed electric utility, the Cooperative Electricity Supply Society Sircilla Ltd. (CESS)
- Scientific partner, the Power Systems Research Centre at the International Institute for Information Technology Hyderabad (IIIT-H)

- Technology partner, the Steinbeis Centre for Technology Transfer, India (SCTI), an expert in technology and knowledge-transfer between research and business
- The advisory committee of two NGOs, the Prayas Energy Group Pune, and the Centre for World Solidarity Hyderabad (CWS)
- The local NGO, Self-Employed Welfare Society (SEWS), which has extensive experience working with farmers, predominantly in the field of watershed management

Subjects, Issues, and Contents

Extensive survey research identified the major drawbacks in the knowledge and education of the farmers. The research results guided the design of the training sessions. Furthermore, a technical survey revealed the most urgent problems with motor maintenance and provided inputs for the training agenda.

Methods, Scenarios, and Organisation

For the different target groups, various training formats have been used. Two different training programmes have been developed for the farmers. The first type of training concerns all farmers and provided a basic introduction to the issues of maintenance of capacitors, motors, pumps, starter boxes, and distribution transformers. The second type of training was comprised of only farmers who have ex-ante knowledge of motors and pumps. They received more in-depth training, which included instructions for small-scale repair work at the pump set level and how to identify poorly maintained distribution transformers. The electricians, (the second target group), received theory-based training of motors and capacitors, as well as instructions on how to install capacitors and conduct measurements.

Instruments, Products, and Learning

The training sessions were conducted by experts in the respective fields. Training material was distributed in the local language and the basic training sessions were held in a straight-forward manner. Many farmers are illiterate and cannot understand written documentation. Consequently, the training material was supplemented by illustrations.

Costs, Efforts, Resources, and Preparation

The training sessions were carried out on a low-cost basis. The farmers themselves organised the training sessions, including provision of space in the village. Once the training sessions have been established and proved to be beneficial to the farmers and the authorities, they should be organised and financed by the farmers and CESS.

Essential Requirements

One major requirement is that farmers are willing to participate—up to now this was not always the case. The initial phase required extensive groundwork. In this specific instance, farmers were encouraged to form Distribution Transformer Committees (DTRCs). Social mobilisers were employed to assist the formation. Furthermore, the technical intervention—installation of capacitors—helped to capture the interest of the farmers.

Experiences

The training sessions were only a small measure within the pilot project, but proved to be one of the most important parts of the implementation. Incorrect maintenance of starter boxes and capacitors led to an increased number of capacitor failures. Additionally, many farmers were suspicious about capacitors. Farmers linked the increased number of burnouts with the newly installed capacitors. These misconceptions could be clarified after the formation of DTRCs and training sessions.

The causes for burnouts are often difficult to track and may create a skewed perception of the intervention.

Fig. 6   Basic farmers' training at a DTRC in Namiligundupally village [Malte Müller]

Fig. 7   DTRC members in front of their transformer [Malte Müller]

Implementation

The training was conducted in the following order: firstly, a training session for the electricians was conducted. They learned about the basic functioning of a capacitor, how to install it, and how to measure relevant parameters. In a later training session, they were instructed to train the farmers in basic concepts of motors, pumps, and capacitors. Subsequently, the electricians trained the farmers in DTRC meetings. The advanced training sessions for farmers who had a technical background were held one month later. By then, a basis for further training on different subjects—such as better water management—had been established.

Transfer and Dissemination Activities

The training sessions were very specific and adjusted to the requirements of the pilot project. However, the major implications are valid for a broad field of applications. The basic findings suggest that top-down approaches do not work, as farmers stop supporting them. Therefore,

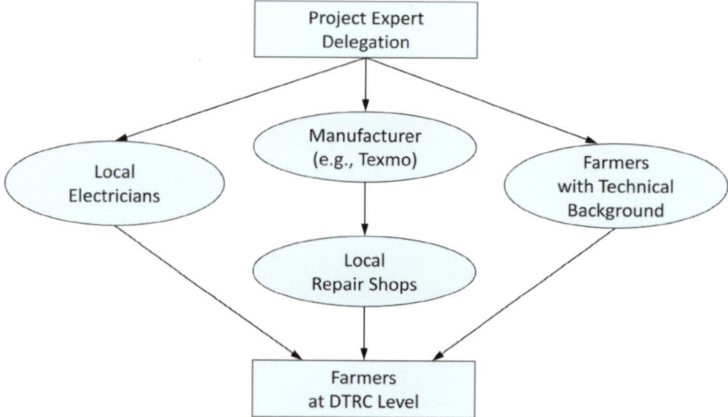

Fig. 8   Schematic diagram of trainings [Authors]

Fig. 9   A burned starter box [Malte Müller]

Fig. 10   Farmers' gathering with officials from the CESS [Malte Müller]

it is important in many projects that deal with rural development to involve the local population. The most effective way is to involve farmers in decision-making processes and to train them on what they might be able to do to improve their situation. The concept of the training was presented to the electricity regulator. After a final evaluation, the aim is to transfer the project to other areas of the state. The concept can be transferred to regions where farmers face problems with electricity quality. This is the case in many developing countries, including Africa and South America.

For more Information

General information about the Sustainable Hyderabad project is available at:
http://www.sustainable-hyderabad.de

about the pilot project at:
http://www.sustainable-hyderabad.de/implemation/pilot-project.html#PP5

and about the Megacities programme of the German Federal Ministry of Education and Research at:
http://future-megacities.org/

For more detailed materials like training guidelines, please contact the authors.

TEHRAN-KARAJ: Reconstruction of a shipping container as construction training room [Nadia Poor-Rahim]

Nadia Poor Rahim, Bernd Mahrin

Mobile Learning Containers (MLC) for Improving the Qualification of Workers at Construction Sites

Keywords

Mobile Learning Room
Vocational Training
Practical Construction Training
On-site Training
Unskilled Workers
Qualification
Modular Training Centre

Basic Information

Location: Islamic Republic of Iran, Tehran-Karaj Region/Hashtgerd New Town
Climate: The climate in the Tehran-Karaj region is semi-arid.
Geomorphology: The region is heavily endangered by earthquakes.
Ecology: The population's awareness about energy and environment has not yet achieved a desirable level. As result, any efforts have to be supported by education and awareness-raising measures.
Population: Iran's population rose from 67 million inhabitants in 2003 to 80 million today. Of these, 15 million live in the Tehran-Karaj region and 50,000 in Hashtgerd. More than two-thirds of the Iranian people are under the age of thirty.
Education: The literacy rate is 82%. Women compose more than half of the university students. The general education system has improved enormously during the last three decades. Vocational training is strongly focused on academic knowledge and theoretical issues, whilst practical training is commonly disregarded.
Employment: According to official figures, the number of unemployed fluctuated from 12 to 14% in the period 2009–2013 [Statista 2014]. The actual number is probably much higher.
Economy: The economy is dominated by central planning, state ownership of oil and large enterprises, village agriculture, small-scale private retails, and service ventures. Infrastructure has been improving steadily during the past decades, although it is currently affected by inflation and unemployment. The inflation rate was more than 30% in 2012 and now has a slightly downward trend. The service sector contributes about 47% of the GDP, followed by industry (mining and manufacturing) with 42% and agriculture with 11% [Tandem 2008].
Governance: There are strong national efforts to increase environmental protection and sustainability, to care for ecological necessities, to reduce greenhouse gas emissions, and

to halt the waste of resources. The subsidies for oil, gas, electricity, and water have been rigorously decreased.

Resources: With nearly 4,000 barrels per day, Iran is the world's fourth largest oil conveyor country. Indeed, the capacity of the refineries in the country lags far behind the crude oil production, so that predominantly crude oil is exported and refined products have to be reimported.

Initial Situation

Energy efficient and high-quality construction are not only important for the environmental and climate impact of new satellite cities, but also for the economic success of the construction industry as a key industry in Iran and in other countries of the region. The often devastating effects of frequent earthquakes could be significantly reduced with the professional realisation of construction with skilled workers, and according to appropriate building codes [Saghafi 1998, 2004]. Based on available Iranian earthquake studies and on the author's own construction site visits and expert discussions, a broad analysis of construction faults was compiled in the Young Cities Project. It demonstrates that a significant portion of structural damage results from improper workmanship, which is partly based on lack of necessary qualifications [Mahrin/Meyser 2013]. A high demand for practical training has been consistently requested by experts for many years [Naficy/Khallaghi 2003, Saidi 2003]. The following images impressively clearly show that these demands have not yet been fulfilled.

Due to inadequate attention to existing building codes, accidents with severe injuries often occur at construction sites. Also, due to insufficient knowledge of planning and bad construction work, the energy efficiency of buildings is generally very low. Frequently, fluctuating construction site staff also exacerbate the problem. The best way to deal with the problem and to get quick improvements would be to qualify the workers individually, taking their experience and their assigned tasks into consideration. This, of course, is not really a sustained education, but only functional training for a specific job. Nevertheless, step-by-step, it can lead to broader competencies and to opportunities for the workers' career development.

Constructing a "New Quality Building" as planned in pilot project of the same name, requires skilled workers in several disciplines on the operational level [Rückert et al. 2011]. These are, for example, bricklaying, reinforced concrete steel construction, tiling, plastering, insulating, installing housing technology, drywall construction, etc. The construction management staff should be made up of highly skilled foremen and their assistants who have a high level of practical experience, in order to guide and control the complex processes of different tasks. These briefly summarised facts were determined by analysing the few available written sources, interviewing Iranian experts, managers of the Iranian Ministry of Labour and Social Affairs, as well as visiting the training centres in Hashtgerd, Karaj, and Tehran, construction sites, as well as having discussions with their employees [Schmidt/Mahrin 2013].

Special Background

Gainful employment as a worker in the construction industry is frowned upon in Iran and other countries in the region. Vocational training, or even partial qualifications are not common in this industry. The academic training of civil engineers and architects is at a high level, but their practical construction experience remains insufficient. Even in larger companies, the percentage of experienced and permanent labourers in the construction sector is low. Not only the realms of educational and training have deficiencies, but additional problems are also created due to inadequate social security, low status for construction workers, poor working conditions, low wages, grim employment outlook, inadequate safety at work, and labour migration.

Objectives and Targets

The overall objective of the Young Cities supplementary project, Mobile Learning Containers (MLC) is to enable vocational training in each upcoming work process. Short workshops can be held alongside the construction site in order to impart at least a basic knowledge and experience of professional construction work. Mobile learning containers can provide a suitable base for this activity. Of course, not all of these "quality barriers" can be eliminated by a single measure like providing MLCs. It is also necessary to develop complementary changes. But developing and implementing MLCs can be an important step towards gaining more technical competence at construction sites, leading to durable and energy-efficient buildings [Meyser/Mahrin 2013].

A significant part of the learning process should be implemented in practice and on specific jobs directly on construction sites. In terms of a practice-theory connection, the basic technical background, material properties, etc., have to be taught; execution alternatives will be envisaged and practised. For these purposes, a venue to learn and practise is needed

where models, printed material, presentation boards, notebooks, digital learning equipment
(videos, images, process simulations, etc.), and minimal technical equipment, including a
workshop area are available. Such a place rarely exists on construction sites and, moreover,
the necessary learning support facilities are certainly unavailable.

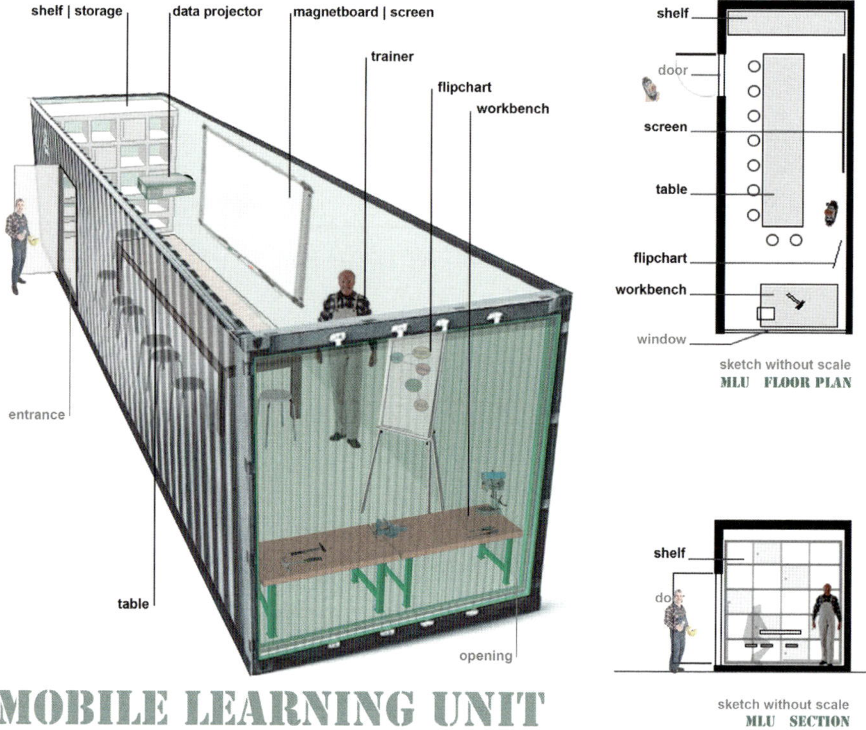

Therefore, a mobile, flexible, reusable, and adaptable solution is required. This unit can be realised in the form of containers. The following figure shows a concept study that should lead to the specification of a prototype model [Mahrin 2013].

The project's primary aim is to create a prototype model and then to test it. The effect of the activities to improve the qualification structure—in other words, the creation of a suitable learning place close to construction sites to enable practical vocational qualifications—will arise gradually, but perceptibly. An encouraging example was the construction of the above-mentioned New Quality Building in Hashtgerd New Town. As a result of upgrading the qualification of construction workers, regular supervision of experts, and using well-proven material (almost without additional technical equipment), the primary energy demand and CO_2 emissions could be halved merely through detailed planning, professional preparation, and proper workmanship [Naeiji/Rückert 2012].

Target Groups

The main target group of the MLCs are:
- Construction companies can organise the work processes in order to let their employees attend in training courses and workshops in close proximity to their workplaces. Ultimately, they will benefit from the courses when the workers have acquired their skills and knowledge and produce a better quality in less time than they were previously able to do.

- Technical and vocational training centres and training service providers can offer and run short training courses at changing places, on small constructions sites, and even in small towns without any vocational training infrastructure.
- Construction workers can participate in training courses according to their interests and needs. This may lead to better job opportunities and to permanent jobs in the construction industry.

Parties Involved

The lighthouse project, Mobile Learning Containers in the framework of the Young Cities Project will be performed by two cooperating departments of the Technische Universität Berlin (Subject Didactics Construction and Landscaping, Prof. Dr. Johannes Meyser, and Design and Building Construction, Prof. Ute Frank). Close coordination with further relevant partners is provided during the MLC project. The (re)construction and equipping of the prototype model will be provided by one of Germany's leading supra-company vocational training centres, the Vocational Training and Technology Centre of the Chamber of Crafts Osnabrück-Emsland-Grafschaft Bentheim. Close cooperation in the design and testing phase and precise coordination with partners in the selected destination country, such as China[1] or Egypt is intended.

Subjects, Issues, and Contents

Steel containers are already frequently used for accommodating classes in isolated and remote areas and as additional space at existing schools and training centres in case of capacity bottlenecks. At many construction sites, preassembled containers are used as offices. Therefore, the most important innovation of the MLC is not the actual use of the containers themselves, but the idea of enabling the implementation of a reasonably priced, elementary, ready-for-use and effective learning infrastructure at construction sites wherever it may needed. The conditions and necessities vary from site to site. Thus, the development of a prototype ought to be seen only as a first step towards the development of modularised training spaces consisting of a variable number of interchangeable containers, each with different functions and equipment. Finally, it should be possible to compose a complete vocational training centre of several units using the open space between for diverse purposes. However, the lighthouse project MLC has to concentrate on realising a single learning container to be as flexible and multifunctional as possible. The prototype will be based on the common commercial transport container, in order to be transportable and flexible for locations.

Case studies at Iranian construction sites [Mahrin/Meyser 2013] prove that a considerable number of employees of construction companies suffer from a lack of job-related training. On-site training provides an important step towards having a skilled labour force if it adequately combines practical training and experience and theoretical background. Therefore, MLCs equipped with models, tools, and teaching materials should be placed directly at the construction site or in close proximity to it. Although there may be a short distance to the workplace, it can still be perceived as an integral part of the entire construction site arrangement.

At private and informal construction sites, the decentralised mobile units can offer consultancy and advice for contractors and agencies, and also to qualify the construction workers. The MLC prototype model will have the following significant characteristics:

- It will be based on a standard 20-ft shipping container and will be transportable.
- It will be used as a learning space and, due to the visible installations, it will likewise serve as a learning prototype.
- It will mostly have self-sufficient supplies and will be independent of site connections.
- It will offer sufficient space for a study group of six people—in exceptional cases up to eight people. One special variant is planned with an extendable sidewall to offer more flexible space, while nevertheless keeping it compact and transportable.
- It is designed as a modular system. Thus both are possible: a "one container solution" for small sites and a combination of study room, shop floor, and storage space for larger sites. In any case, basic and complementary equipment for the joint use of outdoor areas will be provided.
- It is designed and will be produced as a complete, flexible learning space including all technical supply installations, flexible furniture, and educational media, learning materials, and necessary tools for practical construction training courses as requested.

Because even comprehensive research did not lead to comparable concepts, the protection of application rights will be checked in due time.

Methods, Scenarios, and Organisation

The necessary MLC equipment has been identified by expert interviews, case studies, and site visits. The equipment of the MLC prototype will focus on reinforced concrete, external thermal insulation composite systems (ETICS), accelerated aerated concrete (AAC), floating floor slabs, installation of insulated windows and doors, and plumbing seals. During the concept phase of the Mobile Learning Containers, a workshop for architecture students was held in the summer semester 2012 at the Technische Universität Berlin by Prof. Ute Frank from the Department of Architecture together with her research assistant, Andrea Böhm. The results of this research led to different design ideas that were customised to the specific needs and

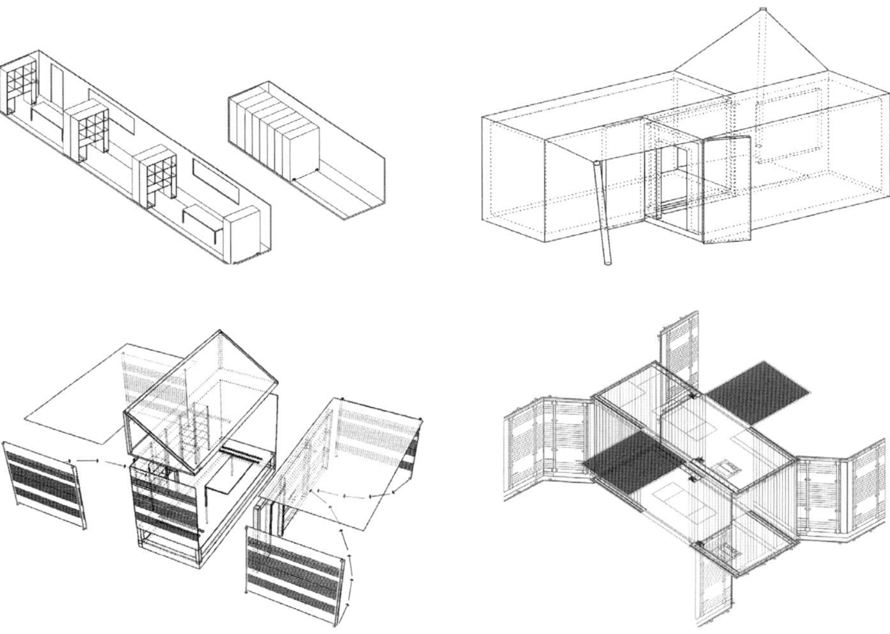

conditions of the different sites and to the corresponding Mobile Learning Container [Böhm/ Frank 2013]. The technical conditions in accordance with building code requirements are to be clarified and thereafter, the exterior and the interior design, as well as the functionality will be adjusted.

Moreover, a feasible plan will be prepared for the energy supply and control via a photovoltaic system on the roof, lighting, thermal insulation, heating/cooling, including the calculation of heating and cooling needs. The technical infrastructure will be exposed as far as possible, so that the features can be observed and understood. This way, the learning unit will become a learning object as well. Didactic function models will be used as supplementary tools, offered by various German educational and technology manufacturers. Year-round usability of the prototype model in the semi-arid countries of the MENA region (Middle East and Northern Africa) is to be ensured. The measures required to regulate the interior temperature and climate, should be designed as energy-efficiently as possible. Construction solutions, such as shading or insulation have to be favoured over installing technical equipment. The containers have to meet three main requirements:

- offer space for learning purposes (i.e., group work, lecture/presentation, practicing, individual work)
- enable practical work with construction materials (workshop room/workshop area/workshop container)
- transport safely and be theft-proof to safeguard the technical and didactic equipment

The construction of the container prototype will be organised as an interdisciplinary process involving different groups—such as experienced engineers and vocational trainers with different professions, apprentices, and university students—in order to directly identify the needs of relevant target groups.

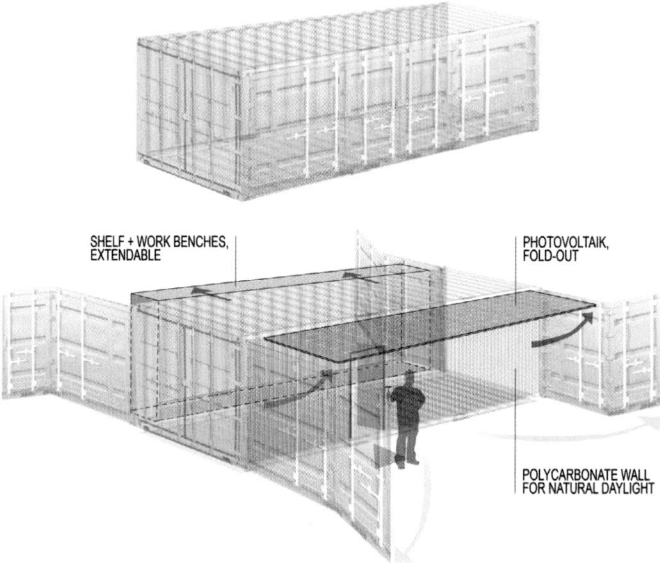

Subsequently, a first trial test will be conducted in Germany and, if necessary, will be repeated with modified MLCs or sceneries. In the final step, the prototype model will be transported to the partner country and will be tested in the anticipated target environment. Subsequently, the experience will be analysed and published.

Instruments, Products, and Learning

The "MLC family" will be designed as a modular and flexible system with the following variants:
- "One-container solution" with the minimum percentage of all functions for small learning groups
- "Two-container solution" with separate teaching and workshop rooms and appropriate interfaces (access/transition, electricity supply...)
- "Three-container solution" with separate teaching, workshop and storage room, and appropriate interfaces (access/transition, electricity supply...)

The choice of the adequate solution depends on the local conditions, the decision of the customers, and their willingness and ability to invest. The prototype model will be designed as a one-container solution as mentioned above.

The interior—which includes the furniture, the technical, and didactical equipment—will be designed as flexible and variable as possible, if necessary in several variations. This is to keep it open for different and changing learning scenarios and to enable various courses and professional needs. The outdoor space should be additionally considered in the use concept; though such use depends on the weather conditions and can only be planned for certain works. The technical facilities will include:
- autonomous electricity supply from photovoltaic cells with batteries as storage, with a generator, and with additional connectivity to site electricity source, if any

- proper electrical installation for construction sites (lights, sockets, distribution/fuse ...)
- compressor for compressed air supply with inside and outside connections
- heating and cooling
- water reservoirs with pump and outside removal option and if possible, for multicontainer solutions inside

Moreover, the MLCs will provide the following educational facilities:

- tables and chairs, cabinets/shelves/roll container, etc.
- whiteboard, projection screen (possibly combined), projector (alternatively LED flat screen), laptops, printers, speakers/headphones
- workbench, basic set of building tools, hand tools, and safety provisions for workers
- a selection of relevant videos, CDs, DVDs, brochures, manuals instructions, technical learning books, and learning materials, as well as functional models and view models

Learning aids and instructional materials are to be stored in changeable and portable boxes. Thus, the container's function can change according to the different themed boxes.

Costs, Efforts, Resources, and Preparation

The project management, construction, material creation, evaluation, and related tasks will be performed by academic staff members of the Technische Universität Berlin. The container itself, the necessary material for the renovation and interior design, the technical equipment, and the transport of the MLC to the partner country will be financed from the project budget, which will be funded by the German Ministry of Education and Research (BMBF). The didactical equipment will only partially be financed from the project budget as some industry-sponsored projects have been promised. The overall cost for the MLC prototype may amount to about 150,000 euro, including all the overheads and development costs, as well as travel and transport costs. Since the previously elaborated concept, including all design documents, can be used repeatedly, the cost of later reconstructions will be significantly lower in comparison with the original prototype model—estimated to be between one-third and one-half of the costs. Providing the didactic equipment may possibly result in a cost reduction. A reliable market worldwide is expected for such modular and flexible learning containers as there is a high demand for work-based training opportunities at construction sites. The marketing concept is to be developed during the project; and is to be provided by industry partners. Parallel to the desired marketing of MLC via educational technology manufacturers, there are marketing options for construction documents and relevant handouts, in order to allow replicas by third parties in destination countries. This will possibly be coordinated with future industrial partners.

Essential Requirements

The mobile learning container should be provided with at least the standard equipment of a small seminar room and, as previously discussed, a collection of illustrative and informative material. Some organisational and financial cooperation is needed to ensure the success of the project:

- cooperation of related organisations—i.e., TU Berlin, vocational training centres, related partners in destination countries, and construction companies
- financial support, not only for design and producing the prototype model, but also for evaluation of the project to improve its function.

Experience

The discussions held with experts in and from Iran, China, Egypt, Brazil, and other countries have shown that the approach of MLCs as a small and flexible learning unit has a far greater chance of being realised and creating opportunities for action than large, stationary training centres. The reasons for this are fourfold:

- Initially there are relatively low start-up costs and comparatively low operating costs to be covered.
- If successful, it can gradually and comprehensively spread upwards.
- The accessibility to potential users is significantly better due to decentralised management and spatial variability.
- In brief, it is possible—even on an hourly basis—to achieve positive results for the construction company through improving quality, and avoiding rework for site-related learning processes. Thus, an immediate return of the investment is probable, in contrast to long-term training sessions in training centres, which companies may not regard as suitable for "short-term staff".

Implementation

Via the implementation and the trial operation of the MLC, the key aspects of the very successful short-course training workshops on construction sites would be achieved. This can be realised with far lower cost, and less effort; moreover, positive outcomes for implementing much larger training centres will appear. Some German vocational training centres have expressed their interest in constructing a prototype, fully equipped container with the involvement of apprentices. Participation of the student projects is included, so that a professional and cross-functional cooperation can be formed as a focal part of this project. For this reason, travel costs are incurred.

The project started on 1 July 2013 and will be completed by 31 August 2014 with the first test results in Germany. The following steps are planned:

- detailed planning of container types
- detailed planning of interior design and technical equipment
- detailed planning of teaching and learning equipment
- creating operating concepts, including teaching recommendations, as well as the concept for advisory and agency tasks
- realising the prototype (construction, installation, interior design) with apprentices in a German vocational training centre
- testing in Germany
- evaluation and modifications
- registration for utility model protection
- transportation to a destination country, repeating the issue of the licence there together with the local partners

Transfer and Dissemination Activities

Discussions have already been held with potential users, such as a large construction company in Urumqi/China as a location of one of the BMBF-Megacities projects. Furthermore, there have been talks with experts and construction companies in Egypt and in Brazil. All of them have expressed their explicit interest. Even German companies that produce educational technology for various disciplines conveyed their interest–depending on the variety of their professional marketing activities–either to support the container's equipment, or to cooperate in its global marketing. Similar problems of low construction quality and poor qualification of workers exist in many other developing countries in Africa, Asia, and Latin America. Thus, affordable and flexible solutions are needed to offer the required construction training. Therefore, excellent marketing opportunities from cooperation with expected professional training technology providers can be expected. The implementation of short-term workshops at the construction site of the first large passive house project in western China is planned based on the approved Young Cities Model within the framework of overall project collaboration with the Megacities Project Recast Urumqi.[2] The Chinese partners have expressed great interest in the container-based MLCs and are already able to finance them themselves. In connection with the current Water-Energy-Building, Training and Transfer, WEB-TT[3] in Haram City (Egypt), the Orascom Construction Industries (OCI)– one of the biggest Egyptian construction companies–has also expressed its interest in the concept. Since the company offers the full design and implementation of all settlements including infrastructure in many countries of the MENA region and beyond, the MLC could be a part of each settlement plan, as a part or core of a training structure. Further requests have already come from Kyrgyzstan and Brazil for didactic innovation for learning scenarios alongside the construction site, beyond an economic utilisation perspective, in cooperation with experienced marketing partners for educational technology. Last but not least, use of the containers seems beneficial under appropriate conditions on construction sites in Germany. The appropriated scenarios for this concept will be developed as part of the beta testing in Germany.

References

Böhm, A./Frank, U. (Eds.) (2013): *Architectural Progression # A Handbook–the LIFEcenter in Iran– Building for Vocational Training*. Series competencies and facilities, Vol. 2. Universitätsverlag Technische Universität Berlin

Mahrin, B. (2013): "Mobile Lernumgebungen und Handlungsansätze für die internationale Berufsbildungszusammenarbeit. In: Baabe-Meijer, S./Kuhlmeier, W./Meyser, J. (Eds.): *Perspektiven der beruflichen Bildung und der Facharbeit*. Ergebnisse der Fachtagung Bau, Holz, Farbe und Raumgestaltung. Norderstedt, Books on Demand, pp. 148–72

Online: *bwp@Spezial 6 - Hochschultage Berufliche Bildung 2013, Fachtagung 03*. http://www.bwpat.de/ht2013/ft03/mahrin_ft03-ht2013.pdf

Mahrin, B./Meyser, J. (Eds.) (2013): *Construction Competencies and Building Quality–Case Study Results*. Young Cities Research Paper Series, Volume 06. Universitätsverlag Technische Universität Berlin

Naficy, A.-H./Khallaghi, A.-A. (2003): *Technical and Vocational Education and Training in Iran*. Iranian Ministry of Education (Ed.), Third Revision, Tehran

Rückert, K./Grunwald, J./Mahrin, B. (2011): "Pilot Project New Quality". In: Schäfer, R./Nasrollahi, F./Ohlenburg, H./Stellmacher, F. (Eds.): *Accomplishments and Objectives*. Young Cities Research Paper Series, Volume 02. Berlin, Teheran. Universitäts¬verlag Technische Universität Berlin, pp. 90–94

Schmidt, K/Mahrin, B. (2013): "Results of Construction Site Visits and Expert Talks". In: Mahrin, B.; Meyser, J. (Eds.): *Construction Competencies and Building Quality–Case Study Results*. Young Cities Research Paper Series, Volume 06. Universitätsverlag Technische Universität Berlin, pp. 20–27

Saghafî, M.-J. (1999): "Survey of the Damages Resulting from Execution Deficiencies in Buildings Damaged by the Ghaenat Earthquake, May 1997". In: *Honar-ha-ye Ziba—Fine Arts, Architecture and Urban Planning*, Volume 4 & 5, pp. 62–72.

Saghafî, M.-J. (2004): "Damages resulting from defective construction and supervision processes in Bam earthquake, December 2003". In: *Honar-ha-ye Ziba—Fine Arts—Architecture and Urban Planning*, Volume 17. pp. 43–52

Saidi, K. (2003): *Iranian National Masterplan for a Labour Market Orientated Job Training System*. Discussion paper, Tehran, GTZ

Naeiji, K./Rückert, K. (2012): *Analysing Energy Performance of New Quality Building Envelop by Computer Simulation*. Contribution to the IGC Cologne—32nd International Geographical Congress, 26–30 August 2012, Cologne

Notes

1 See the essay "Training on the Way to the First Passive House in West China" by Franke et al. [pp. 131-140 ↗] in this volume.

2 For more information, visit: www.urumqi-drylandmegacity.uni-hd.de

3 For more information, visit: www.web-tt.org

TRAINING PRACTICE AND THEORETICAL INSTRUCTION

HYDERABAD: Food vendors are omnipresent in the streets [Carsten Zehner]

Anne Dahmen, Christoph Dittrich, Mamidi Bharath Bhushan

Integrating Street Food in a Sustainable Food Distribution System—Food Safety Training for, and with, Street Vendors

Keywords

Street Food Sector
Food-safety Training
Hyderabad
Food Vendors

Basic Information

Location: India, Andhra Pradesh (AP), Emerging Megacity of Hyderabad

Ecology: Climate change is predicted to lead to extreme weather events, disastrous floods, heat waves, extreme droughts, and increasing water scarcity.

Population: (Hyderabad Metropolitan) 7,749,334, Population growth (decadal): India 17.64%; AP: 11.1% (Census of India 2011). "Greater Hyderabad", a fast-growing metropolitan region in Southern India, will reach 10.5 million inhabitants by 2015.

Economy/Living Standard: Approximately one-third of the population lives below the poverty line and continues to suffer from severe food and health problems. The emerging megacity experiences rapid economic growth enabling higher living standards and modern lifestyles for the emerging middle class. This is, however, accompanied by escalating energy and resource consumption and constantly increasing greenhouse gas emissions per capita.

Governance: The core modules of analysis in the project follow the hypothesis that "getting the institutions right" is one main key to solve the problems of sustainable resource use in general and sustainable demands on climate and energy in particular. Whether or not a society will be able to cope with the impact of climate change and increased scarcity of energy depends on its capacity to change human behaviour. This requires changing institutions, defined as "sets of rules" and governance structures, i.e., those "modes of organisation" that are necessary to put rules into practice.

Project focus: The project's main subjects are climate and energy in a complex transition process towards sustainable mitigation and adaptation strategies by changing institutions, governance structures, lifestyles, and consumption patterns in Hyderabad. Given the natural, social, and economic context of the emerging megacity, the question arises: what can be considered a reasonable response to the anticipated climate change impact? This is the guiding research question of the project. In order to try and answer this question, it was necessary to explore greenhouse gas mitigation and adaptation strategies and ways towards increased energy efficiency and renewable energy.

Initial Situation

Climate change is a significant and emerging threat to megacities and to Hyderabad's food security system. One option that can contribute to mitigating the impacts of climate change and to lower greenhouse gas (GHG) emissions is to address a decentralised and resource-efficient urban food provision system.

Empirical findings reveal that strengthening existing structures of urban micro-retail could contribute to a more resource-efficient and sustainable city development [Dittrich 2008; Rani and Dittrich 2010]. The street food sector (food items that are directly prepared and consumed on the street) in particular show great potential for fostering sustainable development, not only in the ecological, but also in the economic and social dimension. This highly decentralized food distribution system provides affordable, nutritious, and culturally accepted food items tailored especially to the needs of poorer and lower-middle-class dwellers. It operates on the basis of resource efficiency, low waste output and low GHG emissions [Bhushan, Dahmen, Schulz and Dittrich 2013]. Street food also provides a flexible yet profitable source of income, especially for those who do not fit into the formal economy [Rani and Dittrich 2010].

To unleash its potential for sustainable development and integrate the street food sector in modern urban development, several problems have to be solved and challenges met. Street food has often been regarded as backward, out of date, associated with health hazards and traffic obstructions, and as not fit to meet the ends of modern urban development. Due to legal constraints, the majority of street vendors work without a licence, which often leads to corruption demands, arbitrary displacements, and the confiscation of their belongings.

The pilot project Sustainable Street Food Plan (SSFP) is a conceptual framework for practitioners and policy makers based on research findings and outcomes of best-practice activities [Figure 1 ↗]. It conceptually integrates key elements of a decentralized, low-emission urban food provision system with the issue of food security and normative concepts of climate change mitigation. It focuses on options for meeting challenges and facilitating the strengthening of the existing street food system of Hyderabad and unleashing its potential for sustainability in mega-urban development. The capacity building measures presented are just one component of a much wider range of best-practice activities [Figure 1 ↗].

Special Background

The Sustainable Street Food Plan (SSFP) is comprised of four pillars. The best practice activity Street Food Safety Manual and Training, which is our focus here, corresponds with the food safety component of the pilot project. It also touches on issues of the other pillars—for example, the legal situation of street food vendors.

Studies reveal that food safety standards in the street food sector can be regarded as similar or even better compared to other eateries in Indian cities [Neeraja 2006]. Most vendors run their business with great care: food items are freshly prepared in front of customers; ingredients are prepared on a daily basis; and leftovers are uncommon. Food contamination is only rarely observed.

Nevertheless, the hygiene-and-safety discourse—maintained by restaurant, supermarket, and food-court owners—further harms the public image of the street food sector and suppresses recent discussions on improving the legal situation of the vendor community.

However, street food is prepared under special conditions. The lack of cooling facilities and running water as well as exposure to high levels of air pollution require special measures to ensure food and beverages sold on the street are always safe to consume.

India's latest Food Safety and Standards Act [FSSA 2006, amended 2011] has included petty vendors for the first time. The implementation and registration of street food vendors under this act is a realistic option for street food vendors to obtain legal certainty. In Hyderabad (one pilot city among eight selected cities in India), about 1,200 of approximately 18,000 street food vendors had obtained their registration certificate by the end of 2012.

The Institute of Preventive Medicine (IPM) has been assigned by the federal government to issue these registration certificates, and implement and control the FSSA regulations in the petty trade sector. This includes all street food vendors.

This certificate must be renewed annually. However, interviews in the vendor community have shown that even registered vendors were not at all aware of the FSSA regulations, and are therefore at risk of losing their registration certificate.

Objectives and Targets

The best practice activity Food Safety Manual and Food Safety Training for Street Vendors, within the framework of the pilot project Sustainable Street Food Plan, aims to achieve the following objectives:

- Improve food safety standards in the street food sector by raising awareness and supporting capacity building measures through education, campaigns and training
- Develop and provide appropriate training material
- Provide suitable information and guidelines to incorporate into vendors' daily routine
- Enable vendors to consciously follow the requirements of the Food Safety and Standards Act [FSSA 2006] in order to obtain their registration as petty food businesses
- Enable vendors' associations and cooperatives to provide capacity building measures within their group (training of trainers), to easily spread knowledge and skills independent of state authorities.

Target Groups

The street food vendor community of Hyderabad is the target group for the street food safety training. Vendor groups, such as vendors' cooperatives, serve as a platform to sensitise and mobilise vendors to participate in training and set up a group of active members who can be trained as trainers.

The educational and social backgrounds of street food vendors are as diverse and complex as the street food sector itself and the way it works.

Street vendors may belong to migrant communities, recently arrived in the city—often from other Indian states—with mother tongues different from Telugu, the spoken language of Hyderabad. Or vendors are part of families running street food businesses in the city for generations.

Formal education is usually very limited. Many young people with little formal education enter the street food business. Or, as is also common, vendors have studied up to class ten, and have in some cases even obtained a higher degree. Both groups often start to work in the street food sector because they do not fit into the formal economy [Rani and Dittrich 2010].

The vast majority of the vendors involved in activities of the capacity building project are sending their children to school or even college. The latter is true especially for families working in the street food business for more than five years. However, participants of the pilot training—the majority of them being above the age of thirty-five—have often not been able to read and write the local language, either because of the lack of formal education or because of their migrant background.

Parties Involved

In-depth consultations with street food vendors during interviews and group discussions have been one of the most essential undertakings to tailor the content of the manual and other training material to the needs and skills of the target group. A *Street Food Safety Manual* was compiled in cooperation with different stakeholders working on the issue of food safety and street food.

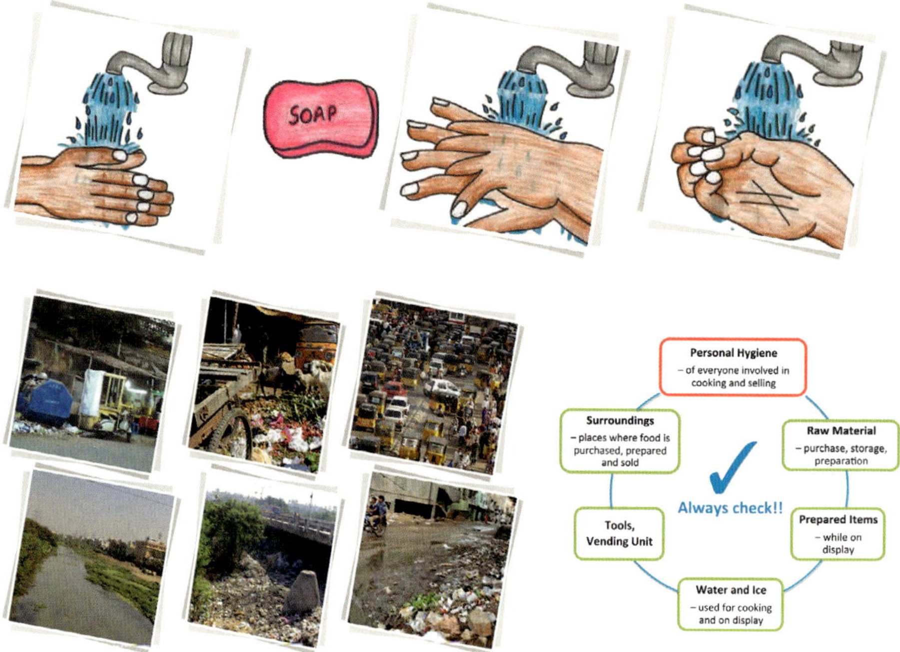

NGOs that have worked with street food vendors for many years provided a well-established network to access organised vendors. In the case of the pilot project, street food vendors' cooperatives have been established with the support of an NGO. These groups provided a platform to mobilise vendors to become food-safety trainers and participants of the pilot training programmes.

Subjects, Issues, and Contents

Through the manual and its utilisation during food-safety training, vendors gained basic information on food safety and hygiene issues, such as the purchase of safe and healthy raw materials, energy-efficient food preparation, safe handling and storage, personal hygiene, appropriate locations, upgrades of vending units, as well as waste-reducing practices.
The main emphasis regarding the compilation of materials is to provide information that is tailored to the special roadside conditions of street vendors and approved by local experts, but is still easy to understand and practical to apply. Moreover, it should improve existing food safety standards.
The manual and other training materials are tools for enabling the transfer of skills and knowledge to street food vendors. This material is used to train selected members of the vendor community to become certified food-safety trainers. These trainers act as peer leaders in their community to sensitise, raise awareness, conduct training, and follow the regulations of the Food Safety and Standards Act. The food-safety training is combined with the registration process, a precondition of legal certainty and the most crucial objective in the process of restructuring and modernising Hyderabad's street food provision system [Figure 6 ↗].

Fig. 6 A food inspector and a food-safety trainer examine the cooking utensils of a street food vendor during a field excursion [Dahmen, 2012]

Methods, Scenarios, and Organisation

Building capacities within vendors' communities: provide, enable, and facilitate. The Street Food Safety Training approach will be briefly described as follows:

In cooperation with street food vendors' cooperatives, the capacity building measures have been carried out during the pilot project phase in 2012 and 2013. These cooperatives operate as legal and institutional organisations, providing services like savings accounts, advocacy, and mutual support. Experienced cooperative society members were selected and trained to become certified food-safety trainers. These trainers act as multipliers within their communities.

Training of Food-safety Trainers (six days)

Besides German scientists, the teaching team consists of local experts of different scientific and practical backgrounds—for instance, nutritionists, municipal food inspectors, and NGO activists.

Days 1–3: Provision of training material and information on hygiene and nutritional, business and legal aspects to future food-safety trainers. Didactic concepts such as group work, peer learning, and discussions in the classroom are complemented with excursions to visit

Fig. 7   Training of Trainers 2012–Peer learning, trainers discuss the training schedule [Dahmen, 2012]

Fig. 8   Training of Trainers 2012–Expert input by Dr. T. Neeraja, Home Science College, Hyderabad [Schultz, 2012]

a sample of vending units in order to discuss food-safety issues on the spot during vendors' daily routine.

Days 4–6: Enabling future trainers to teach with confidence. Information on teaching methods, compilation of class schedules, try-outs [Figure 9 ↗], and many additional practical exercises were part of the classes. After the six-day training seminar, the food-safety trainers received their certificate.

The next step was to mobilise the vendor community to participate in four days of food-safety training camps. In January 2013, about eighty vendors received training and their attendance certificate.

The education of trainers and the capacity building of vendors were accompanied, supervised, and monitored by a group of experts to supplement the capacity building measures with their experience and to detect and correct minor inconsistencies in the course of the training sessions [Figures 7 and 8 ↗].

Fig. 9   A future food-safety trainer during his first presentation [Dahmen, 2012]

Fig. 10   First groups of street food vendors being trained on food-safety issues [Schultz, 2012]

Instruments, Products, and Learning

Apart from learning in a classroom setting of up to twenty vendors and giving them space to discuss individual matters, on-site training was very valuable in the process of the participants' understanding. At least one day of the four-day training seminars was held at the roadside vending unit. Practical challenges (e. g., traffic air pollution) and solutions (optimal way to cover food items, reduction of waste, etc.) could be discussed in depth. Vendors could also be asked to apply their newly acquired knowledge and to refer to challenges in practical implementation.

Costs, Efforts, Resources, and Preparation

The mobilisation of vendors to participate in the training seminar was the biggest challenge during the entire process of capacity building. Street food vendors, who work about ten to fourteen hours every day, fear income losses while attending full-day training sessions. Therefore, it was essential to assess what time of the day a vendor could possibly be called for training and to schedule training in time slots according to vendors' convenience. This and other organisational questions were covered in a survey during the preparation period training in Hyderabad. According to this survey, four-day training seminars seemed convenient to the vendors. The food-safety training seminars also had to be specific enough to match the various local street food cuisines with their specific food-safety challenges. We concentrated on the most important ones: the Chaat, Tiffin, Chinese fast food, and snack food cultures.

Apart from the compilation of materials, the financial costs of conducting these capacity building measures were moderate. Vendors who received their capacity building and food-safety trainer certificate received INR 1,000 in financial compensation per day (approximately 13 euro) for those days when they offered training to their colleagues. The team that supervised, monitored, and supported the programme did not necessarily need to work full time during the preparation or implementation phase. Local NGOs with staff trained in food and nutrition issues have to support the vendors' group in order to organise and conduct training seminars.

In the case of Hyderabad, the experts participating in the training of trainers and the supervision process did so free of charge. Further programmes should provide a budget for this purpose. The costs of renting space, chairs, etc. for classroom training as well as catering (tea and snacks) were low and nearly negligible.

Experiences

Although food-safety training certainly plays an important role in ensuring the legal certainty of food vendors, it is not the most prominent topic for vendors. In the vendors' perspective, the constant harassment—for example, by traffic police—and the persistent fear of being evicted and losing equipment and income are rarely connected to food-safety and hygiene issues. Hence, to call vendors for training seminars often requires convincing them of the advantages of attending this capacity building measure. Therefore, the first training day is especially designed to approach this issue. Nevertheless, the dropout rate in the pilot has been about 10%. But, interestingly, many of the dropouts from the first training group enrolled for the second group training due to the positive experiences and outputs of those who successfully completed the seminar.

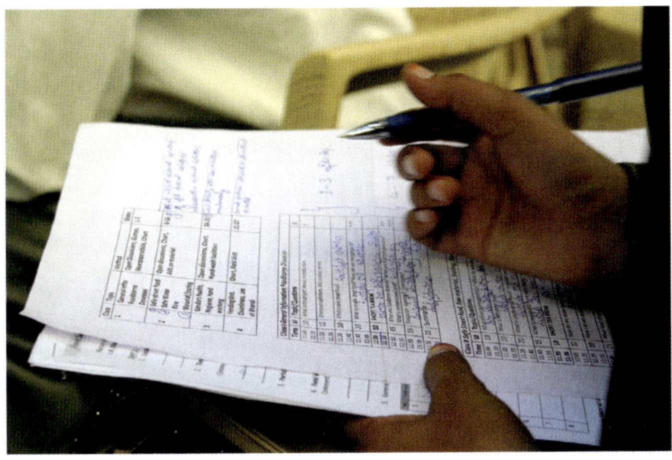

Regarding the awareness of street vendors of hygiene standards and their practical implementation, the food-safety training was of great success. One major obstacle, however, has been the constant harassment by the traffic police. Bribes are often collected on a daily basis. Registering vendors and issuing the certificate of food-safety training are the responsibility of the Food Safety and Standards Authority, a federal government body. In contrast, municipal traffic police—unaware of the schemes of these authorities—do not acknowledge the new legal position of street food vendors and keep threatening vendors with evictions. Hence, strengthening legal support for street food vendors remains the biggest challenge in order to sustain the positive impact of programmes like food-safety training.

In this regard, a positive impact of the pilot project activity is the increasing number of street food vendors joining the cooperative societies. This will strengthen their negotiating position in the debate on ways and means to legalise and modernise the street food system in the emerging megacity of Hyderabad.

Implementation

Why train vendors to become food-safety trainers?

Contact between municipal stakeholders enforcing food-safety standards and the street vendors' community has been highly tense in the past for various reasons. Our studies revealed communication gaps between food inspectors and vendors. This was closely observed when accompanying food inspectors during their daily inspection tours. Routines and individual realities of street food vendors usually do not match the picture drawn in the regulations of the governmental standards. When regulations have been violated, food inspectors can issue penalty fees [GoI 2009]. Often, the inspectors did not explain to the vendor the actual problem; nor could the vendor obtain practical advice on how to change the situation for the better.

Training street food vendors to act as food safety trainers within their community provides the chance for a more practical application of the given standards. Bridging the communication gaps and putting the focus on solutions that are fit for real-life situations have been a proven impact of the pilot training.

Why work with food vendors' cooperatives?

The capacity building measures have been closely linked to vendors' communities. Street vendors are organised to a very limited extent, which makes it difficult to call meetings and inform them about activities. Street food vendors' cooperatives provide a promising option to gain access to, and work with, individual vendors. Regular street-food training will also strengthen the "service portfolio" of the cooperatives and contribute to their acceptance. These cooperatives also hold the potential to act as representative bodies of the street vendors.

For more Information and Products

Manuals in English and Telugu and other information material are ready for download at www.uni-goettingen.de/de/426536.html.

References

Bhushan, B. M./Dahmen, A./Schultz, S./Dittrich, C. (2013): *Environmental Audit of Street Food Vending in Hyderabad—A Study*. Research Reports for Analysis and Action for Sustainable Hyderabad, Berlin

Dahmen, A./Katukuri, S./Neeraja, T./Dittrich, C. (2012): *Street Food Safety Manual. A Training Tool for Hyderabad's Street Food Vendors*. Hyderabad, www.uni-goettingen.de/de/426536.html

Government of India (GoI) (2009): *National Street Vendors' (Protection of Livelihoods and Regulation of Vending) Policy*. Ministry of Housing and Urban Poverty Alleviation (MOHUPA), Delhi

Food Safety and Standards Authority of India (FSSA) (2011): *Food Safety and Standards Regulations 2009, amended 2011*. Delhi http://www.fssai.gov.in/Portals/0/Pdf/Food%20safety%20and%20Standards%20%28Licensing%20and%20Registration%20of%20Food%20businesses%29%20regulation,%202011.pdf

Neeraja, T. (2006): *Capacity Building Project On Street Food Services. Phase III. Action Research on Street Food Safety and Quality with Special Reference to Mobile Food Vendors in Hyderabad*. World Bank assisted CBP on Food and Drug Safety, Unpublished project report, Hyderabad

Rani, U./Dittrich, C. (2010): *Options to Improve Food Safety in the Street Food Sector of Hyderabad*. Research Reports for Analysis and Action for Sustainable Development of Hyderabad, Berlin, www.uni-goettingen.de/de/209108.html

ADDIS ABABA: The IGNIS project supports different waste management initiatives [Lukas Born]

Andrea Schultheis, Dieter Steinbach, Haimanot Desalegne, Mekuria Gebru

Waste Management—Practical Training and Capacity Building

Keywords

Practical Composting Training
Theory of Constraints
Video Films
Manuals
Addis Ababa
Waste Management
Practical Waste Treatment
Charcoal Production
Paper Recycling

Basic Information

Location: Addis Ababa, the capital of Federal Democratic Republic of Ethiopia
Climate: The air temperature is fairly constant throughout the year, with variations between 20°C and 25°C during the day and between 7°C and 11°C at night. Average rainfall is 1,200 mm per year, with the major rainfalls occurring between July and September.
Geomorphology: With an elevation ranging from 2,200 to 2,800 m above sea level, Addis Ababa has a topography consisting of hills, valleys, rivers, and streams.
Population: 86 million inhabitants in Ethiopia, thereof about 4 million in Addis Ababa, which is one of the fastest growing cities in Africa.
Living Standard: Services such as piped water, electrical lighting, and other facilities attracted migrant populations from other parts of the country. In addition to this, the rate of rural-urban migration drained rural labour forces from agricultural production into the city. This created problems of unemployment, congestion, and strains on the inadequate existing infrastructure in Addis Ababa.
Economy: Addis Ababa is the main trading centre for coffee, the country's chief export, and for tobacco, grains, and hides. The major industries produce food, beverages, processed tobacco, plastics, chemical products, textiles, and shoes. In addition, the city is the centre of the nation's service and financial sectors. Addis Ababa has a growing tourism industry.
Governance: Unlike the African cities of colonised countries, Addis Ababa is characterised by its spontaneous growth as an indigenous city with very little impact from external forces. The city has begun to develop as a political, economic, and cultural centre in the near future. It is a quite modern city, hosting the headquarters of the UN Economic Commission for Africa (ECA), the African Union (AU), and a large number of embassies, consulates, and other international organisations. From this point of view, Addis Ababa is the diplomatic capital of Africa.

Fig. 1   View of Addis Ababa [Authors]

Initial Situation

The problem of inadequate infrastructure applies also to the waste management sector. Waste management in a rapidly growing city requires adapted planning and technical solutions. The capacity building measures were conducted with the objective of providing theoretical and practical knowledge on different waste treatment options. The focus was to demonstrate that waste can be a resource and to show how to use this resource in an economically and ecologically beneficial way, particularly with a view to generating income.

Waste management in Addis Ababa involves different stakeholders—such as the administration/waste agency, waste collectors, youth and women's groups dealing with waste collection, treatment, and recycling, entrepreneurs in waste businesses, NGOs, and those in academia responsible for study courses dealing with waste management. All of these stakeholders have only a limited know-how about useful and adapted waste technologies and how to handle the increasing waste streams in a sustainable and environmentally sound way with existing limited financial resources.

Background in the Fields of Culture and Education

Waste collection in Addis Ababa is of high priority. Some years ago the city was about to lose its title as the "Capital of Africa". Heaps of uncollected waste in the streets made the city unrepresentative of this title. The city council reacted and introduced hundreds of youth groups to collect waste from households, markets, etc. This was an effective measure and today,

Fig. 2   Waste collection backlog [Authors]

Fig. 3   (left) Waste collection from market [Authors]

Fig. 4   (right) Women's group producing charcoal briquettes [Authors]

Fig. 5   TOC expert from South Africa [Authors]

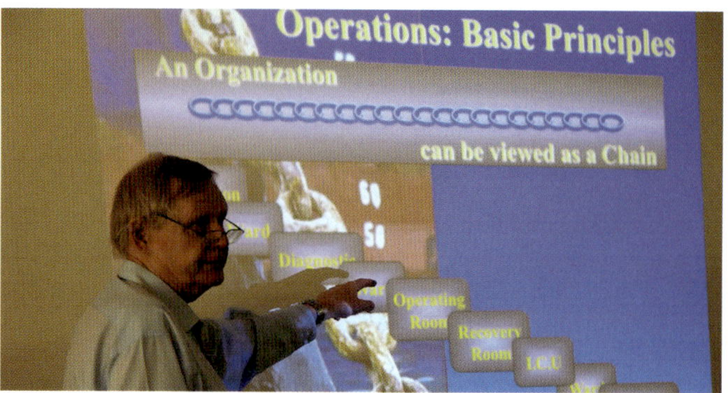

compared to many African cities, Addis is quite clean. Nevertheless, there are still collection backlogs and about 30% of the waste remains uncollected.

Most of the groups dealing with waste are now officially registered and paid by the local city administration. They collect waste from households and transport it to central collection points, from where the containers are then transported to the dump site by the city council. Regulations and ordinances on waste treatment have not yet been introduced. There is no fee system available that guarantees a reliable financial basis for waste management. Recycling and the treatment of organic waste are in place only for a small portion of the waste. This is due to a lack of technical background, practical knowledge, and expertise. Waste management planning with a view towards future city development—including the economic aspects, logistics of transport, useful recycling and treatment options, and knowing the specific advantages and disadvantages of different systems—is still in its early stages.

Objectives and Targets

The general target of the capacity building measures was to raise awareness and demonstrate that waste treatment—even on a small scale—can provide useful options for waste management planning, and that waste treatment can also be a source of income. This requires capacity building not only in theory but also in practice. The practical training and demonstration aspect is very important, as seeing practical operations and results usually create a better educational impact on stakeholders than any written document.

The practical training on improved waste management could not start from one day to the next. Prior to beginning the training, small-scale pilot facilities were installed, such as a composting facility and charcoal production. In addition, a small-scale paper recycler became a practical training example in the project. Waste management, practical waste treatment, and waste business are dependent on each other. Therefore, the target was to improve the management skills of the involved administration and skills in practical waste treatment and business operations of youth and women's groups and the paper-recycling entrepreneur.

Target Groups

In order to give fruitful impulses to the waste management system in Addis Ababa, the capacity building measures were not focused on one group alone. They included different target groups, such as the city administration—particularly the waste authority and the Environmental Protection Authority (EPA)—university assistants, NGO staff, and practical waste workers (youth and women's groups). The practical training, such as on composting, was intended for youth groups and staff from EPA, NGOs, and the Addis Ababa Institute of Technology (AAIT), who participated to learn and then to apply and replicate what they have learnt. Participants from different target groups attended the specific workshops for the city administration as well. This contributed to a clearer common understanding amongst the workshop participants about the different tasks and potential underlying problems and conflicts.

Parties Involved

Project researchers developed training programmes on practical waste treatment for composting, charcoal production, and other waste treatment options. They also worked out the training

proceedings and conducted practical training. Capacity building using the Theory of Constraints (TOC) as a training method—particularly for the women's group and the paper recycler who intended to start a business or improve the business—was performed by team members from the University of Pretoria (South Africa). For the capacity building measures concerning the composting facility, the GORE Company, also a part of the team, provided useful expertise.

Subjects, Issues, and Contents

Experiences during different projects in developing countries showed how important demonstration facilities are to increasing awareness and having a greater learning impact. Written documents, studies, and even manuals often remain stored unread in filing cabinets. The project team implemented the pilot composting plant and charcoal production unit and used a small paper recycling plant as a learning tool. These pilot projects served as theoretical and practical training foundations and provided the background on, for example, market analyses for compost, charcoal, and recycling paper products. The goal was to run these pilot projects as an income-generating and therefore economically sustainable programme beyond the end of the project.

The TOC method was applied with respect to business training, including learning how to do market studies and business plans. The women's groups and the paper recycler were trained using TOC to formulate their business targets and to learn how to reach their goals and identify constraints that prevent them from reaching their goals. For the youth groups that wanted to start a compost business, the focus was on practical training to guarantee high quality compost. The market analysis for compost was performed as part of the overall project.

The TOC method was also applied to different departments of the city administration dealing directly or indirectly with waste. The focus of the training was to obtain a joint analysis with the majority of stakeholders involved for a better understanding of the complex relationships between the different problems related to waste management services and their causes. This included identifying and prioritising constraints that prevent the improvement of solid waste management in the city.

Methods, Scenarios, and Organisation

The training at the composting site comprised two days of theoretical training on biological processes. The five weeks of practical training included a search for suitable sources for the input material, selection of useful materials according to the biological process requirements, waste sorting, windrow building, turning, and sieving, regular analyses (temperature, water content, etc.), and journal-keeping. Around fifty youth (divided into two groups) and staff members from the EPA underwent this training. The training was always half-a-day long because the groups still had to work their regular jobs. Staff from the local NGO project partner also attended the training to learn and to get practical experience, which can serve them in the future as trainers for other groups. Participating assistants from AAIT analysed the transferability of their experiences for study courses at the university.

EPA staff and one of the youth groups started operating composting facilities. For this, it was very important that the trainees understood fully the overall biological processes and each single process step. This allowed them to react immediately when problems occurred during the composting process. During the periods when the team members were out of Addis Ababa, both the youth group and EPA staff were accompanied via e-mail and phone to answer questions and provide advice whenever needed.

Business aspects were the focus of the TOC training for the charcoal-producing women's group (fifteen women). It was challenging to communicate the business basics to the mostly illiterate women. After half a year of operating the charcoal business, a second round was

Fig. 8   Charcoal production video (training film and manual in English and Amharic) [Authors]

Fig. 9   Construction of the composting plant [Authors]

performed for the group to analyse progress and to discuss the results, problems, and constraints, in order to find appropriate solutions.

The intention of the TOC training for the city administration was to discuss future strategies and implementation obstacles.

Instruments, Products, and Learning

Long-term experiences from other developing countries formed the basis for the theoretical composting training. The training was held in the form of a dialogue where the participants had a very active role. The practical training followed an easily understandable, written training manual. In addition, all steps of the training were commented on and documented by means of a video. This provided the possibility that single steps could be recalled easily and practised as often as necessary, even when the trainers were not around.

For the TOC training, the work of the women's group was analysed to tailor the TOC workshop to their needs. Guidelines on how to do a market analysis and business plan for groups and micro enterprises were developed by the project team and used during the TOC workshops.

The TOC for the paper recycler was focused on product quality improvement and product diversification.

For the TOC on the administrative level, the Addis Ababa waste management system was analysed and the stakeholders involved were questioned, and as a result, the demands of the workshop topics were defined. The output of the TOC was documented in the form of a road map providing the next steps of action.

Efforts, Resources, and Preparation

The trainings were imbedded in real facilities that had to be built before starting the training. For the composting, this took several months. This was the same for the charcoal project as the available technology had to be re-engineered before starting the business. Within six months, German students developed simple, affordable, and easy-to-handle technology.

The TOC facilitators analysed the work of the women's group and for the paper recycler two days before preparing the training. The workshop for the women's group was scheduled for one week and the follow-up had the same time requirement. The duration of the TOC for the paper recycler was four days.

Preparation of the TOC workshop with the city administration could be based on the stakeholder analysis, which was part of the general project. Problem analysis within the city administration required contacting the relevant persons and discussing the current problems with respect to waste management. This was the basis for making a final decision on the TOC workshop topic. The time required for the TOC, including preparation and post-training evaluation, was around three weeks.

Essential Requirements

Besides the facilities, technical equipment, workshop room, and consumption materials—which had to be available before starting the practical training—the commitment of the participants was the most crucial requirement. In addition, some financial means were required to support the transportation of participants to the training location and to offer meals and beverages. For the women's group, compensation for loss of production during workshop time was necessary.

Experiences

The training for the women's groups and youth groups was challenging because of the weak educational background of the participants. Moreover, due to political intervention, the trained youth group that operated one of the composting facilities was removed from the composting site and replaced by another group. The new group, made up mostly of elderly people, did not have any interest in starting a composting business and the composting site has been abandoned since then.

For the EPA staff, the composting training was very useful and composting has taken place since then. The NGO staff who attended the composting training is now training further groups, not only in Addis Ababa, but also in other regions of Ethiopia.

In the beginning, the TOC training with the city administration was challenging, as it was the first time that different departments and different administrative levels had to build working groups, and analyse and discuss frankly the constraints of waste management in Addis Ababa without any finger pointing. The special discussion culture made the TOC process slow-moving and not all of the results could be achieved during the workshop.

Furthermore, it was difficult to get the staff, particularly the heads of different departments and different administrative levels, involved in the workshop for more than one day.

With respect to business and market studies for the women's group, the TOC was fruitful—even when the workshop content and layout had to be adapted to the fact that most of the women were illiterate. It became obvious that planning for the future and transferring this planning into a sustainable business concept was a challenging process not only for the participants, but also for the workshop facilitators.

Implementation

The composting project—that is, the facility, the training, and the visible output compost—was successful. Officials from the city administration could convince themselves when visiting the facility that this kind of decentralised waste treatment process could be a beneficial option within the Addis Ababa waste management planning. The result is that two additional composting facilities were installed in other subcities of Addis Ababa, using the same principle learnt during the composting training.

The TOC workshops for the city administration will continue, even beyond the project duration, as the process was seen to be highly beneficial for the waste-management planning process.

The TOC for the charcoal production and paper recycler led to more efficient and business-oriented production, thus providing good practical examples and success stories. Spreading these experiences may contribute to including business and income-generating recycling measures as an option for the city's general waste management planning.

Transfer and Dissemination Activities

Transferring the project results to other rapidly growing cities was an important project target from the beginning. The methods developed, pilot projects implemented, and experiences gained should be transferrable to the conditions of other cities. The idea and method of decentralised manual composting was transferred to a slum area in Nairobi, Kenya. Here, a composting facility was built; separate waste collection was introduced; composting and business training was conducted; and finally, quality compost was produced. This is a successful transfer that will lead to an upscaling to a five- or six-fold input of waste.

Another project is the transfer of the TOC method at the administration level to the city of Lagos, Nigeria. The Lagos waste management department had a special interest in having a TOC workshop on the development of a plan for data collection of waste characterisation. With 160 participants and a detailed roadmap as an output, the workshop was very successful and will be followed by practical action.

For more Information and Products

General information on the IGNIS project can be found at http://ignis.p-42.net
and on the Megacities programme of the German Federal Ministry of Education and Research at http://future-megacities.org/

Some of the materials, such as concepts, training papers, TOC approach, and results, are available for download at http://ignis.p-42.net

TEHRAN-KARAJ: On-site construction workshop [Bernd Mahrin]

Karen Schmidt, Bernd Mahrin

On-site Construction Workshops in Iran

Keywords

Practice Workshop
Short Workplace Seminars
Mobile Teaching Facilities
Dynamic, Image-based Teaching Materials
Unity of Theory and Practice
Recognition of Manual Work
Quality of Construction
Skills Development
Site Management

Basic Information

Location: Islamic Republic of Iran, Tehran-Karaj Region/Hashtgerd New Town

Climate: The climate in the Tehran-Karaj region is semi-arid.

Geomorphology: The region is heavily endangered by earthquakes.

Ecology: The population's awareness about energy and environment has not yet achieved a desirable level. As result, any efforts have to be supported by education and awareness-raising measures.

Population: Iran's population rose from 67 million inhabitants in 2003 to 80 million today. Of these, 15 million live in the Tehran-Karaj region and 50,000 in Hashtgerd. More than two-thirds of the Iranian people are under the age of thirty.

Education: The literacy rate is 82%. Women compose more than half of the university students. The general education system has improved enormously during the last three decades. Vocational training is strongly focused on academic knowledge and theoretical issues, whilst practical training is commonly disregarded.

Employment: According to official figures, the number of unemployed fluctuated from 12 to 14% in the period 2009-2013 [Statista 2014]. The actual number is probably much higher.

Economy: The economy is dominated by central planning, state ownership of oil and large enterprises, village agriculture, small-scale private retails, and service ventures. Infrastructure has been improving steadily during the past decades, although it is currently affected by inflation and unemployment. The inflation rate was more than 30% in 2012 and now has a slightly downward trend. The service sector contributes to about 47% of the GDP, followed by industry (mining and manufacturing) with 42% and agriculture with 11% [Tandem 2008].

Governance: There are strong national efforts to increase environmental protection and sustainability, to care for ecological necessities, to reduce greenhouse gas emission, and to halt the waste

of resources. The subsidies for oil, gas, electricity, and water have been rigorously decreased.
Resources: With nearly 4,000 barrels per day, Iran is the world's fourth largest oil conveyor country. Indeed, the capacity of the refineries in the country lags far behind the crude oil production,
so that predominantly crude oil is exported and refined products have to be reimported.

Initial Situation

One of the most important goals of the Young Cities Project is to minimise the CO_2 emissions
of new buildings. To do so, new technologies and methods for designing the building façade
and the detailing are required. But the appropriate use of new construction materials and
other materials is also of central importance. The aim is to increase the life expectancy of
buildings by improving the quality of construction work, thus considerably reducing unnecessary emissions of greenhouse gases caused by having to erect new buildings prematurely.

Inspections of construction sites at the beginning of the project in March 2009 immediately showed that there is a considerable need for training of construction workers. There is
a great discrepancy between the stringent requirements for structures and the skills of most
construction workers. As in many countries, training in Iran is very theoretical. Only a few of
the construction workers have had any practical experience with similar construction projects.
Most are unskilled and are migrant workers from poorer countries in the region. Training is
made more difficult by cultural differences, language barriers, and lack of literacy skills.

Another obstacle is access to high-quality construction materials and tools. Our research
revealed that, although many of these products are available, the necessary information is
lacking and the sources have not been adequately explored. Producers and suppliers are only
gradually beginning to make information widely available. Improvements in the advertising
and use of Iranian construction materials and tools would be advantageous.

Background in the Field of Construction

Construction work is very unpopular in Iran. The opportunities to obtain an apprenticeship or even a low-level qualification in this branch are completely inadequate. A significant lack of communication between construction-site management and workers is evident. Highly skilled foremen or site foremen with extensive experience are not permanently present, especially at smaller sites. Most of the architects and construction engineers have an excellent theoretical background, but not enough practical experience. Therefore, the mainly unskilled workers receive hardly any professional instruction and support.

There is a significant lack of awareness of energy efficiency, as well as a lack of appropriate qualifications, even amongst foremen and construction workers. Although energy-efficient construction is formally required by official building regulations—especially by the so-called Code 19—it is often ignored by building owners and construction staff.

The working conditions for unskilled workers—often immigrants from Afghanistan, Iraq, Pakistan, or other countries—are hard. There is no permanent employment, insufficient social security, and inadequate safety at work.

A link between site-management and construction workers comparable to the foreman (*Meister*) or supervisor in Germany is not common in the Iranian construction industry. Experienced practitioners with management skills are rare on Iranian construction sites. However, they would be central to achieving buildings of a high standard.

Objectives and Targets

The principal aims of the Young Cities pilot projects were to increase energy efficiency and greatly reduce the emissions of buildings compared with the usual levels in Iran. Individual projects focused on improving the quality of structures, on conception and design improvements, or on the use of new technologies and materials. In each case, it was necessary to

Fig. 4 Practice workshop in Hashtgerd New Town: External thermal insulation composite system (ETICS) [Navab Motlagh/TU Berlin]

Fig. 5 Practice workshop in Hashtgerd New Town: Floating floor [Navab Motlagh/TU Berlin]

raise the participants' awareness of these issues and to give them the skills required to tackle them. The participants were also meant to act as communicators and pass on their skills to others.

We started with the skills workshops, which were held at the model construction site of the first pilot project that was done. This was the New Quality Building in Hashtgerd/Iran, a residential building with sixteen units. It was possible to achieve a marked improvement in the standard of construction thanks to the experienced instructors from the Vocational Advancement Service of the Berlin-Brandenburg Construction Industry Association (Berufs-

Fig. 6   Practice workshop in Hashtgerd New Town: Masonry work with AAC blocks (autoclaved aerated concrete) [Navab Motlagh/TU Berlin]

förderungswerk e.V. des Bauindustrieverbandes Berlin Brandenburg e.V.), who not only professionally taught sound workmanship in the various building trades, but also passed on their experience. The workshops also dealt with new methods and technologies. Above all, they focused on construction practice. This instruction was supported by short theory sessions on the technical background, held in seminar facilities nearby.

The topics for the short workshops were agreed in advance with the Road, Housing & Urban Development Research Center of Iran (BHRC, former Building and Housing Research Center).

Target Groups

The workshops were designed principally for the personnel who were working directly on the construction site—the majority of whom were unskilled construction workers—and to a lesser extent for the construction engineers at management level.

At the request of the Iranian project partners, the training programmes were also adapted to suit target groups comprising site managers and scientists.

The Iranian construction engineers showed a great deal of interest. University courses do not include any practical elements. Consequently, practical construction skills are weak and there was a great deal of interest in the practical instruction given by experts. However, the construction engineers and architects were largely reluctant to take part in hands-on exercises. This is because it is unusual for them; in addition, their culture views manual construction work as being unsuitable for academically trained construction engineers.

Parties Involved

The workshops were prepared by two instructors from the Vocational Advancement Service of the Berlin-Brandenburg Construction Industry Association (BFW BB) in Germany and held in Tehran and Hashtgerd with the support of the BHRC and the Housing Investment Company. Both instructors had many years of practical experience in building construction and have been involved in vocational training for construction workers for a long time. They were supported by a construction engineer from the Technische Universität Berlin (TU Berlin), who supervised and documented the construction of the New Quality Building. Academic staff from the Department of Vocational Training and Education at TU Berlin played a leading role in developing the concept for the courses and their evaluation. An Iranian-German colleague from TU Berlin and an Iranian colleague at the BHRC acted as translators during the courses.

A total of one hundred Iranians attended the theory and practice workshops held in Tehran and Hashtgerd in January and February 2010. Most of the participants were construction engineers and site managers. Foremen and construction workers attended the practical demonstrations and exercises. Fluctuations in participation were possible as the workshops were structured as short sessions dealing with specific topics. The fact that many of the construction workers attended the practice sessions but not the short theory sessions, while many of the engineers attended only the theory sessions, revealed the differences in attitudes of the Iranian and German participants towards the need for training.

Subjects, Issues, and Contents

The first series of seminars held in Iran in January and February 2010 lasted two weeks and comprised a total of eight workshops dealing with specific topics. The theoretical and practical components were taught either directly at the site of the New Quality Building in Hashtgerd, in nearby seminar facilities belonging to the developer or, in some cases, in the BHRC's seminar facilities in Tehran. The principal topics were as follows:
- Use of autoclaved aerated concrete
- Plastering and rendering
- Installation of windows and doors
- Floating floors
- Sealing joints in sanitary facilities
- Laying tiles in thin-layer mortar
- External thermal insulation composite systems.

The following aspects were covered for each topic:
- Terms and definitions
- Physical principles in construction
- Material properties and regulations concerning the use of materials
- Working procedures
- Choice of tools
- Structure and comparison of various systems
- Alternative solutions
- Health and safety in the workplace
- Error analysis and how to avoid mistakes
- Practical tips.

Fig. 7   Practice workshop in Hashtgerd New Town: Mounting stainless steel anchors in an AAC masonry wall [Navab Motlagh/TU Berlin]

Fig. 8   Practice workshop in Hashtgerd New Town: Gluing insulation panel [Navab Motlagh/TU Berlin]

Methods, Scenarios, and Organisation

Before beginning with the series of seminars, the German instructors familiarised themselves with the local situation. When visiting the construction site of the New Quality Building, they reflected on how they had performed such work in the past. Many of the tools that they would normally use were not available on the construction site. The instructors visited numerous suppliers of construction materials and tools in Hashtgerd and Tehran, where they unexpectedly found several of the tools that were needed, even though the suppliers were often not sure what they were supposed to be used for. Anything that was not available was produced simply by the instructors with the aid of the BHRC.

After clarifying the range of participants expected at the workshops, which was only possible after arrival, some modifications were made to the concepts for the workshops and learning scenarios that had been developed in advance. Thus, the methods used in individual teaching sequences and the content of the sessions were adapted as much as possible to suit the expectations and needs of the heterogeneous target groups, taking into account the skills that needed to be developed and the participants' practical experience with construction work.

The basics were taught in the theory workshops, which were well attended, with the aid of digital presentations and information materials, such as product datasheets and rules for the use of materials drawn up by the producers of construction materials in Germany. Samples of materials—such as corner profiles and waterproofing tape for external thermal insulation composite systems—which the instructors had brought with them, gave rise to interesting discussions on possible uses and alternative solutions.

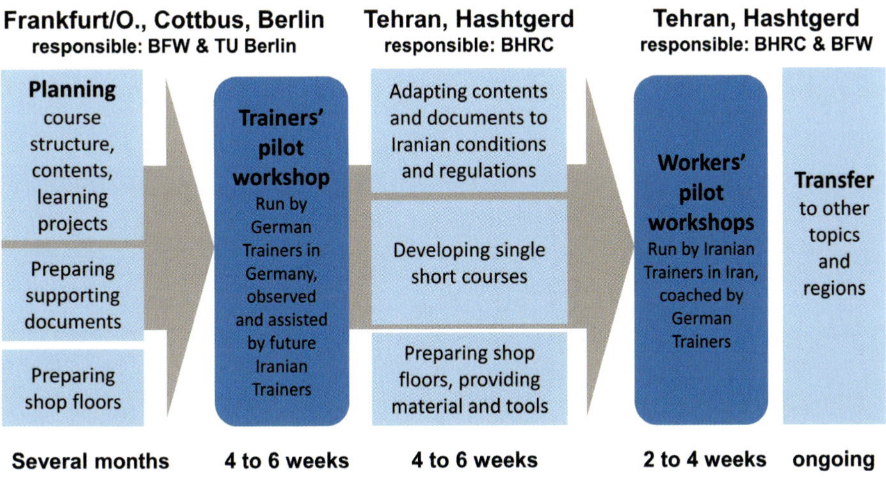

In the subsequent practice sessions, the instructors demonstrated the various working procedures on the construction site and helped participants to put these into practice by performing practical exercises in the actual building. There was a lively exchange of experience between the Iranian foremen and the German instructors. This was a departure from the way in which training courses are traditionally organised and a new experience, especially for the Iranian colleagues. Thus, it was possible to address and discuss fundamental problems with regard to the available construction materials, such as characteristics, quality, and dimensional accuracy. The participants and instructors alike attempted to find solutions to minor problems on-site straightaway.

Instruments, Products, and Learning

The numerous visits to construction sites and the resulting catalogue of damage in concrete and reinforced concrete construction, energy-efficient building, welding, installations, and site equipment formed the basis for preparing the workshops. The catalogue covered a total of eighty instances of damage, with descriptions of each individual case, including proposals for possible repair solutions [Mahrin/Meyser 2013].

At the request of the Iranian partners, a three-stage basic concept for training of trainers was developed ("Road Map") [Figure 10 ↗]. A period of three to four months in total was scheduled for training. The aim was to provide a basis for the subsequent training of site personnel in Iran by Iranian instructors/trainers. In addition, the technical details of the concept were elaborated for concrete and reinforced concrete construction by way of illustration.

The plans for implementing the concept, which was to begin with an introductory phase in Germany followed by adaptation and test phases in Iran, turned out to be unrealistic, as the Iranian trainers were unable to obtain travel permits and funding. This meant that it was not possible to implement the Training of Trainers concept within existing Iranian educational structures. However, in the end it was also possible to reach the target group with the short workshops. Further development of these activities is strongly recommended—and is the intention of the Iranian partners—to allow positive results to be achieved in the long term.

Preferred Executions, Techniques, and Materials

Basements/Foundations	Strip Foundation	Bottom Slab (spread foundation)	Special Foundation (e.g. piled foundation)	Others	Remarks
Support Structure	Steel Skeleton Building	Reinforced Concrete Construction	Brick Lining Material	Others	Remarks
Ceiling	Monolithic Reinforced Concrete	Concreted Filigree Elements	Prefabricated Elements	Others	Remarks
Wall Construction	Brick Masonry	AAC	Reinforced Concrete	Other Material	Wall Structure — single-leaf / double-walled

Special Characteristics (Lintel Types, Special Bricks, Installation Bushings)

Wall Thickness	Outside Walls	Interior Walls	Load-Bearing Walls	Non-Load-Bearing Walls	Remarks
Wall Coating	Plaster	Tiles/Panels	Wallpaper	Wooden Sheathing	Others	Remarks

Simple image-based learning aids were produced to support the unskilled and inexperienced workers in the learning process and with working procedures on the construction site. These included:

- Printed instruction sheets in English and Persian in which the working procedures were explained simply and in easy-to-understand terms, with numerous images and little text, and
- A dynamic online learning programme with videos showing how to correctly carry out key, frequently recurring working procedures.[1]

An interview guideline [Figure 11 ↗] was drawn up to analyse situations on the construction site, substandard workmanship, and the subsequent need for training. It is an aid for recording situations on the construction site and their context—client, budget, site equipment, occupancy of the building, legal specifications, building services, etc.—as well as for deriving topics and goals for online workshops adapted to suit specific situations. Both the guideline and the instruction sheets can be downloaded free of charge at www.youngcities.org/137.html

Costs, Efforts, Resources, and Preparation

The first workshop in Iran lasted two weeks. The preparation time required by the instructors and the effort involved in coordination must also be taken into account. The overall cost of this pilot scheme was around 12,000 euro. This included personnel costs and travel, food, and accommodation expenses for the two German instructors, as well as the cost of translation and interpreting services and printing the seminar scripts.

The overall cost depends to a large extent on the amount of preparation and follow-up work involved, and therefore decreases considerably when seminars are repeated. The workshops described above were pilot schemes with the clearly defined objective of enabling Iranian communicators to continue, establish, and propagate such training courses in Iran in the future. The organisational effort and financial cost would then be reduced to a fraction of what was originally required. However, this transfer requires considerable efforts to be invested in the technical and didactic preparation of the communicators. It also requires practical training to be valued more highly. The Young Cities Project was only able to take initial and regionally limited steps towards achieving this aim.

Essential Requirements

The framework conditions for the systematic preparatory training of construction workers in Iran are inadequate as far as both quality and quantity are concerned. Therefore, it is initially only possible to work in a particular region, with a distinct focus on key training needs in specific areas of work. This is the only approach that is likely to be successful. It requires a valid analysis of needs during the preparation phase and suitable teaching rooms close to the place of work for the practical and theoretical phases of implementation.

Even improvised teaching areas on the construction site are far more effective for the activities described here than central teaching facilities located far away from the construction site. Informational materials on the construction elements and materials used on-site and on the effective use of available tools and aids are minimum requirements.

For example, suitable teaching and learning materials, samples of materials, tools for demonstration purposes, models, and other practical items, in addition to dynamic digital teaching media, could be kept in construction-site offices or in teaching containers that can be easily transported from one construction site to another. A suitable learning space could also be set up in this way with minimum effort.[2]

However, this is only the physical framework for on-site workshops. Success depends above all on the instructors who act as communicators. Highly experienced German instructors worked on the pilot workshops so that the necessary skills were available and only language and intercultural barriers needed to be overcome by mutual recognition. However, a certain number of communicators first need to be trained to enable such training courses to be made widely available. Based on the experience so far, this could best be achieved by stable, medium-term collaboration as part of the transnational cooperation established during the project.

Experiences

The participants at the workshops varied greatly according to the topics being dealt with and the focus on practical work. This was possible as the content of each workshop was clearly defined. Thus, the situation in the teaching groups changed frequently.

This was a new experience for the instructors and adjusting to a new set of participants each day meant that they had to be very flexible. One experience that was new and very important for the Iranian participants was the close link between theory and practice. Building on the theoretical foundations that were taught, it was possible for the practical implementation to be demonstrated and practised straightaway in the practice workshops. Conversely, any questions that arose during the practical exercises could be clarified in the theory sessions when it was not possible to deal with them comprehensively in the practical phases.

One important realisation for the German instructors was the low status of construction workers in Iranian society. If workmanship enjoyed greater recognition amongst all those involved in construction—clients included—workers were better paid, and more effort were put into teaching skills, experience has shown that the standard of construction work would also improve significantly.

There are many highly qualified construction engineers in Iran. Staff members with many years of professional experience are also employed in the middle level of construction-site management in large construction companies. Each of these groups could act as a link between construction workers and site agents. They would be able to greatly improve communi-

cation—which is currently poor—between the different status groups and act as communicators for vocational training. However, they would need to have adequate practical experience, which they could only gain by carrying out such work themselves. The necessary practical components could be integrated into university education and additional communicators could be taken from the resulting pool.

The Iranian Ministry of Labour is aware of the need for future sound vocational training in the field of construction. At this point, close collaboration with the Ministry of Education is both recommended and necessary. Existing vocational training should be jointly examined to determine its effectiveness and be supplemented by successful and innovative approaches, such as the on-site workshops. This is absolutely undisputed by experts in construction and vocational training. However, as there are currently strict political limits on the extent of any German-Iranian cooperation, such developments only seem possible inside Iran at this time.

Implementation

Several Iranian construction companies have expressed a great interest in further workshops with practical components adapted to suit their specific needs. The BFW BB is currently holding talks on this matter with several Iranian companies.

Following the workshops in January and February 2010, a further workshop was held by one of the instructors at the request of the BHRC at the opening of the New Quality Building in July 2010. Topics such as autoclaved aerated concrete, external thermal insulation composite systems, and waterproofing were discussed in a theory workshop attended by around one hundred participants. Some of the participants indicated that there was an urgent need for other workshops of this kind to be held directly on construction sites. Again, engineers accounted for the majority of participants at this workshop.

The teaching media, such as instruction sheets, case studies, and the online-learning platform, are available and can be disseminated in Iran.

Transfer and Dissemination Activities

A workshop on the construction of passive houses in practice was held at the Centre for Sustainable Construction in Cottbus (Kompetenzzentrum für Nachhaltiges Bauen Cottbus, BFW BB) in November 2012. The most important topics discussed were the correct installation of windows and the application of a 30-cm-thick layer of thermal insulation [Figure 13 ↗]. The participants were site managers and other staff from middle management at a large Chinese construction company that wishes to build a passive house with a surface area of around 7,000 m² in Urumqi (in north-western China). The German instructors will assist with work in China and locally train two groups of construction workers in these tasks.

For more Information and Products

Some general information on the Young Cities Project can be found at www.youngcities.org; information on the vocational training approaches is available at www.youngcities.org/137.htm, with some of the materials, such as concepts, training papers, instruction sheets etc., available for download;

and information on the Megacities programme of the German Federal Ministry of Education and Research can be found at www.future-megacities.org.

An interactive online learning tool supporting vocational training for the above-mentioned subjects/issues is available at www.bau.moderntrain.de.

The case study results have been published as a book [Mahrin/Meyser 2013].

Additional products (detailed concept for container-based Mobile Learning Container and others) are available as printed reports. Please contact the authors.

References

Heise, U. (2010): "Iran und seine Baustellen sind eine Reise wert". In: Berufsförderungswerk e.V. des Bauindustrieverbandes Berlin Brandenburg e.V. (Eds.): *Bildung konkret* 1/2010, 2

Mahrin, B. (2010): "Fachkräftequalifizierung im Bausektor im Iran. Entwicklung praxisorientierter Aus- und Weiterbildungskonzepte im Rahmen eines Megacities-Projekts". In: *BWP* 39(2010)6, pp. 49–52. (ISSN 0341-4515)

Mahrin, B. (2010): "Vocational Education and Training as a Precondition for Quality and Energy Efficiency in Construction—Experiences and Solutions from the German-Iranian Cooperation Project Young Cities". In: *Future Intermediate Sustainable Cities: A Message to Future Generations*. Elain Publishing Company, Cairo, pp. 776–88

Mahrin, B. (2011): "Integrated Approach to Achieve Proper Workmanship". In: Schäfer, R.; Nasrollahi, F.; Ohlenburg, H.; Stellmacher, F. (Eds.). *Young Cities Research Paper Series, Vol. 02, Accomplishments and Objectives*. Universitätsverlag TU Berlin, Berlin, pp. 152–6

Rückert, K./Grundwald, J./Mahrin, B. (2011): "Pilot Project New Quality". In: Schäfer, R./Nasrollahi, F./Ohlenburg, H./Stellmacher, F. (Eds.): *Young Cities Research Paper Series, Vol. 02, Accomplishments and Objectives*. Universitätsverlag TU Berlin, Berlin, pp. 90–4

Mahrin, B. (2012): "La calidad como estrategia de innovación—Quality and innovation Require Worker's Qualification". In: Dichiara, R. O./Lind, P. M. (Eds.): *Simposio Internacional Heinz Hermann Erbe—Recursos Humanos y Technológicos, Generació de Innovaciones y Valor Agregado en las Empresas*. EdiUNS 1ra.edición, Bahía Blanca, Argentinien, 13 p, CD-ROM (ISBN 978-987-1620-83-8)

Mahrin, B. (2012): "Berufliche Qualifizierung für und auf Baustellen im Iran—Ein Beitrag zum energieeffizienten und hochwertigen Wohnungsbau". In: *BAG-Report Bau Holz Farbe* 14(2012)2, pp. 26–30. (ISSN 1869-7410)

Mahrin, B./Meyser, J. (2013): *Construction Competencies and Building Quality—Case Study Results*. Young Cities Research Paper Series, Volume 06. Universitätsverlag TU Berlin

Notes

1 Cf. article "Complementary Digital and Printed Learning Media to Construction Topics" by Mahrin [pp. 131-140 ↗] in this volume.

2 Cf. article "Mobile Learning Containers (MLC) for Improving the Qualification of Workers on Construction Sites" by Poor-Rahim/Mahrin [pp. 46-58 ↗] in this volume.

LIMA: The use of treated wastewater has an essential importance for any vegetation in the desert city [Lukas Born].

Artur Mennerich

Wastewater Treatment— International Workshops and Online Learning Platform

Keywords

Distance Learning
Moodle
Urban Water Management
Continuing Education

Basic Information

Location: Lima, the capital of Peru

Climate: Perhaps the most dramatic effect of climate change is the variation in the hydrological cycle, including the melting of glaciers, rising sea levels, and significant changes in temperature and precipitation patterns throughout the world. One of the areas most seriously affected by climate change is the Andean region; there, Peru is the third most sensitive country when it comes to impacts of climate change on precipitation and water availability [Rosenberger 2006]. The shortage of water is expected to be even more severe due to the major intensity and frequency of the El Niño/Southern Oscillation phenomenon. These impacts of climate change are felt not only in the mountainous regions, but actually far more so in the large conurbations, which are characterised by huge demand for water resources. The metropolitan region of Lima and Callao in Peru is a particularly significant example of a conurbation heavily dependent on water.

Ecology: Irregular water supply due to the arid climate (only 9 mm of annual mean precipitation) and irregular flow characteristics (significant seasonal rainfall variations in the Andean mountains, which serve as the main source of water supply).

Population: Lima has a fast-growing population exceeding 8 million, and is considered a megacity. High population growth (annual growth rate of 2%), in particular due to an influx of poorer people, puts additional pressure on those parts of Lima that lack appropriate supplies of electricity, water, and sanitation

Living Standard: The metropolitan area of Lima and Callao is characterised by a number of features typical of emerging megacities. The population of Lima covers all social levels of society. In 2007, 18% of its population was living in extreme poverty. Polarisation between poor and rich districts, with conflicts arising from basic resource availability and a high social mobilisation potential when policies are seen as unfair or putting further burdens on the poor.

Resources: Lima has to draw a major part of its water supply from the River Rimac. Due to the very dry conditions and large seasonal variations in river flow, groundwater is also being used as a source of water supply. Groundwater extraction is in excess of the resources available.

Initial Situation

The conventional approach to sanitation in urban areas, which consists of expensive sewer systems, wastewater treatment in centralised plants, and effluent discharge to the surface of water bodies, is neither an affordable nor a sustainable solution for fast-growing megacities like Lima. The main reasons are:

- The rapid growth of these cities, which makes design and construction of centralised sewer systems almost impossible
- Limited water resources requiring concepts and techniques for wastewater reuse.

In dry-climate regions in particular, the paradigms of wastewater technologies have to change. The main goals will be:

- Identification of simple, appropriate, affordable decentralised sanitation systems and promotion of their adoption
- Implementation of appropriate technologies with the participation of the communities
- Health and hygiene education so that physical facilities can be properly used and maintained, and
- That hygienic behaviour would support the improvements brought about by the infrastructure [Mennerich/Schütze 2009].

Hence, megacities like Lima need appropriate solutions that can be semi-centralised (20,000–200,000 population equivalents connected) [Mennerich/Schütze 2009]. These systems allow for new sustainable possibilities that make use of the resources present in wastewater, i.e.:

- Energy recovery via biogas by anaerobic treatment and its direct utilisation in households
- Reuse for garden or public green irrigation
- Nutrient recovery and application to agriculture
- Separating greywater and blackwater for optimised reuse concepts.

Fig. 2   Auditorium at an international workshop [Author]

Fig. 3   Waiting for workshop participants at the UNI laboratory [Author]

Fig. 4   Lecture at the CIP conference hall [Author]

Sanitation capacity building should see the stakeholders in a sanitation project not as objects, but as partners for developing sustainable sanitation solutions.

Background in the Field of Education

Educational institutions, universities, and technical schools must contribute to the mainstreaming of the new sanitation paradigm by fully integrating the discourse and criteria for sustainability into their curricula. They should make clear that defining criteria for sustainable sanitation is a political act and influences what is considered the accepted, legitimate form of sanitation, including the impacts of sanitation on other sectors.

Therefore, the identification of innovative sanitation technologies and enhancing the education of engineers and technicians to handle these technologies professionally are needed.

Objectives and Targets

Within the LiWa ("Lima Water") project, training and capacity building contribute to general awareness of the actual situation and developments in water management. It provides the advanced application of LiWa results and professional knowledge for students, specialists, and stakeholders to ensure a sustainable water management system that can cope with the impacts of climate change in the coming decades.

Therefore, the aims are to identify innovative sanitation technologies suitable for different representative quarters and the education of graduate students studying these topics. An important objective is the gradual development of sustainable (resource- and energy-efficient) concepts together with stakeholders, decision-makers, and professionals.

Target Groups

Water professionals in public institutions and private enterprises, consultants, students

Parties Involved

- Ostfalia University of Applied Sciences, Campus Suderburg
  http://www.ostfalia.de
- Universidad Nacional de Ingeniería (UNI), Lima, Peru
  http://www.uni.edu.pe
  Jointly, Ostfalia and UNI developed the methods for, and contents of, capacity building activities within the LiWa project.
- SEDAPAL (Servicio de Agua Potable y Alcantarillado de Lima, Peru)
  http://www.sedapal.com.pe
  SEDAPAL, the large operator of water and wastewater systems in Greater Lima, provided technical data as well as organisational support.
- CIP (Colegio de Ingenieros del Perú, Lima, Peru)
  http://www.cdlima.org.pe/
  CIP was the official organiser of the training courses held in Lima. They also provided the conference rooms.

Subjects, Issues, and Contents

For the LiWa project, the Ostfalia University of Applied Sciences (Campus Suderburg) is cooperating with the National Engineering University of Peru's Faculty of Environmental Engineering. Training materials for in-class teaching as well as for distance learning have been developed within LiWa. The contents of these LiWa modules are adapted to specific needs within the project area of Greater Lima, which means that they cover customised technical concepts for larger units in the central districts of Lima as well as more decentralised solutions for the peri-urban areas.

Methods, Scenarios, and Organisation

LiWa uses Distance Learning Lectures (DLL) and Continuing Education Events (CEE) as tools for training and capacity building.

Instruments, Products, and Learning

For DLL, training material is implemented in the e-LiWa-Academy [liwa.ostfalia.de]. LiWa uses this system for teaching at the university and for further education beyond university. The advantage of this system is its availability, regardless of time and location: students and professionals need to have some flexibility in organising their educational timetable, since most of them have one or two full-time jobs.

CEEs are organised as International Workshops for professionals, such as consultants, stakeholders, designers, and others working on water-quality issues.

Costs, Efforts, Resources, and Preparation

The resources needed for creating one distance learning module using Moodle as a platform are approximately as follows:
- 2 PM (person months) for preparing the text (approximately fifty to seventy pages) and additional materials like linking videos and adding photos
- 0.5 PM for translations
- 0.5 PM for creating and checking online tests
- In addition, providing support to students during the online courses requires staff capacity.

Essential Requirements

Internet access for every student; staff for technical support and evaluating student's tests

Experiences

It is not easy to integrate online learning into existing academic curricula.

In this project, one major obstacle for cooperation between Peruvian and German universities was that master's courses in Peru are taken on a part-time basis to accommodate work schedules. That is, courses run in the evenings and on the weekend. Nevertheless, students seem to favour in-person courses where teaching staff is physically present.

Another problem was that, even at the master's level, English courses were not well understood and accepted by the students.

Implementation

In order to extend the capacity building efforts to water professionals, the advanced international workshop "TRATAMIENTO AEROBIO DE AGUAS RESIDUALES DOMÉSTICAS E INDUSTRIALES" for professionals, such as consultants, stakeholders, designers, and others working with wastewater, was offered. This workshop was organised by the LiWa partners, OCS (Ostfalia University of Applied Sciences–Campus Suderburg), and UNI-FIA (National Engineering University of Peru's Faculty of Environmental Engineering), in cooperation with the National Engineering Association of Peru. The speakers were Prof. Mennerich (OCS), Eng. Ogasa (OCS), M.Sc. Yaya Beas (UNI-FIA), Eng. León Suematsu.

The contents of the LiWa modules have been applied in that course. Focal points were, among others: Peruvian/German norms of wastewater treatment; nutrient removal; plant design operation and maintenance; practice in laboratory; and sludge treatment. Sewage plant design based on an example according to the German guideline DWA-A-131, using a demo version of the design software BelebungsExpert, was also included. For this application, OCS translated this software into Spanish.

More than forty participants from all over Peru and neighbouring countries took part. An evaluation showed that this course was very successful.

Transfer and Dissemination Activities

It is foreseen that further courses for professionals will be offered. The distance learning modules will be included in the educational programme of both partner universities.

For more Information and Products

Detailed information and products related to the project are available at:

http://www.lima-water.de

https://liwa.ostfalia.de

http://www.lima-water.de/en/pp6.html.

References

Mennerich, A./Schütze, M. (2009): "Wasser in der Wüsten-Megastadt Lima–Herausforderungen und Ansätze". In: *2. Internationales Symposium Wastewater-Recycling 4.–6. November 2009.* Veröffentlichungen des Institut für Siedlungswasserwirtschaft der TU Braunschweig, Heft 77, pp. 217–22

LIMA: Participants of a summer school [ILPOE]

Antje Stokman, Rossana Poblet, Eva Nemcova

Multidisciplinary Research/Design/ Build Summer Schools: Alternative Solutions for a Water-scarce Future in Metropolitan Lima, Peru

Keywords

Academic Summer Workshop
Design Action
Site Intervention
Multidisciplinary Teamwork
Water-sensitive Urban Design
Prototype Design

Basic Information

Location: The project is located in Lima, Peru, situated on the western coast of the Pacific Ocean. Lima lies between the desert coastal littoral of the Pacific Ocean and the branches of the western Andean slopes, and above the lower watersheds of the Chillón, Rímac, and Lurín rivers. Today, Metropolitan Lima extends over desert, dry hills, and agricultural valleys and is considered after Cairo as the second-largest city in the world located in a desert.

Climate: Although classified as subtropical, Lima's proximity to the cool waters of the Pacific Ocean means temperatures are much cooler than what would be expected in a subtropical desert, and can be classified as a mild desert climate. Average annual humidity along the coast is between 80 and 88%; at higher altitudes it is more than 70% on average, and almost 100% from June through December [Atlas Ambiental 2011]. As a result, during winter the whole metropolitan area is coated with fog that hangs constantly over the city and turns some of the desert hills into temporary herb-rich meadow biotopes called loma.

Geomorphology: Metropolitan Lima's landscape is characterised by four specific landforms and the different processes that shape them: (1) the littoral, characterised by small and medium-height cliffs, beaches and bays; (2) the desert, characterised by a narrow flat area with an average section of 10 km; (3) the valleys, formed by erosive and sedimentary processes due to the flow of the seasonal rivers Chillón, Rímac, and Lurín; and (4) the Andean foothills framing Lima in the west. Because of the steep slope, human occupation is subject to risks. Here, the seasonal ecosystems loma appear due to the concentration of humidity.

Ecology: The main terrestrial ecosystems are coastal lomas, coastal wetlands, endemic cacti, rocky coastline, and fluvial ecosystems. However, the informal urban development has depleted or reduced many of these ecosystems.

Population: 9,585,636 by 2013, according to INEI projections [INEI, 2007]

Education: The literacy rate was 93.44% in 2007 [INEI, 2007].

Employment: Most of the population is employed in the service sector, industry, and agriculture. The unemployment rate was 7.9% in 2011, but underemployment is also widespread.

Economy: The Peruvian economy grew by an average of 6.4% of GDP between 2002 and 2012 [Ministry of Economy and Finance of Peru, 2012]. Despite being considered one of the booming economies in the continent due to its macroeconomic performance, there still exists a large gap between rich and poor.

Resources: Marine resources in the ocean and minerals in the mountainous regions.

Initial Situation

Two summer schools were organised in connection with the pilot project area of the Lima Water research project (LiWa) in the Lower Chillón River watershed, located in the north of Metropolitan Lima. This specific area serves as a demonstration site for the development and implementation of strategies and measures, which address multiple interrelated scales in order to reach the goal of water-sensitive urban development.

Within the research project on the large-scale metropolitan level, the main principles for water-sensitive urban development were defined, harmonised, and integrated into the Lima Concerted Regional Development Plan. At the same time, an analysis of green open space areas was carried out for the whole city in order to understand the distribution and water demands of different types of open spaces. On the meso scale, a Landscape Development Framework Plan for the Lower Chillón River Valley was conceived to guide the demonstration area towards a water-sensitive urban future. On the micro scale, water-sensitive urban design solutions were developed and applied in the design of a strategic project for a linear River Park on the Chillón River.

Temporary installations for low-cost and water-sensitive urban design interventions were built at the summer schools to initiate and communicate the concepts of water-sensitive urban development to the community and institutions. The process and results of the design action summer schools were an integral part of the multiscalar approach of the research activities. Conceptual water-sensitive urban design solutions for different water sources were developed within the open space in the first summer school 2012, while proposals for water-sensitive and eco-efficient public schools were developed in the second summer school 2013.

Fig. 3   People living in informal settlements lack many basic services, including access to potable water and safe sanitation [Evelyn Merino-Reyna Buchanan].

Background in the Fields of Culture, Politics, and Ecology

Migration, population growth, and lack of planning have led to a vast expansion of informal settlements in Metropolitan Lima in recent decades. These settlements lack many basic urban services—such as water supply, waste disposal, and wastewater infrastructure—which have caused environmental degradation. More than one million inhabitants of Lima do not have access to the public drinking water network. At the same time, parks and street greenery have a high water demand and are often irrigated with potable water. The increasing water demand for green areas and the high cost of drinking water put pressure on the wastewater infrastructure, which is informally misused for irrigation purposes with negative hygienic consequences.

In order to put forward a water-sensitive urban design approach, the issue of a disconnection between civil engineering, architecture, urban and landscape design, and ecology was tackled at the summer schools. The provision of basic infrastructure services is typically the responsibility of civil engineers, with the issues of good design and ecology being seen as secondary. This results in urban and landscape design being cosmetically laid over traditional engineering solutions, leading to mono-functional solutions, such as rivers captured in deep concrete channels or slopes sealed with concrete to prevent erosion. Additionally, design professionals ignore Lima's limited water resources: they implement decorative green lawns, flower plantations, and spectacular water parks that consume a huge amount of drinking water and destroy the natural environment.

However, Lima's metropolitan park authority SERPAR is tackling these challenges: in some parks, wastewater treatment facilities have been installed to recycle wastewater for the irrigation of green areas. Still, many of these solutions are facing technical problems, high installation costs, high levels of energy consumption, and high maintenance costs.

Fig. 4 Widespread planting of decorative, water-intensive grass and tree species, together with inefficient irrigation practices, put additional stress on limited water resources [ILPÖ, 2011].

Fig. 5 The primary aim of the summer schools was to develop design solutions that overcome the current disconnection between people, urban landscape, and available water resources [ILPÖ, 2012].

Objectives and Targets

The objective of the summer schools was to engage students from different backgrounds on the issue of water scarcity and pollution, by developing and implementing creative ideas to solve problematic urban situations and creating new opportunities and amenities for the public.

The main challenges that were tackled by the students during the summer school were as follows:

- What types of green areas can be developed in a desert environment?
- How can water be reused for the sustainable irrigation of green areas?

Fig. 6 Students from different disciplines worked together to develop a holistic design solution [ILPÖ, 2013].

Fig. 7 The task of the summer schools was to design and build a strategic semi-permanent intervention on-site, which involves local inhabitants and local knowledge and has the highest potential for being adapted and further developed by the community and authorities [ILPÖ, 2012].

- Which types and how many green areas are needed in the urban setting to provide a playful, educational, and attractive environment?
- How can green areas not only be beautiful but also contribute to the provision of healthy food and to the purification of dirty water?
- How can children, teachers, and the community be involved in developing their environmental awareness and enable long-term project sustainability?

A holistic integration of the urban water cycle, urban landscape, and people can only be achieved through transdisciplinary cooperation between different disciplines. Therefore, the main target of the summer schools was to bring together students, academics, public and private institutions, as well as local residents of the chosen project area, in order to initialise the dialogue and cooperation needed for sustainable solutions.

Target Groups

The main target groups of the summer schools were German and Peruvian bachelor's and master's students from different disciplines—including architecture, landscape architecture, spatial planning, agricultural engineering, sanitary engineering, wastewater sanitation, and social sciences. The students worked in mixed groups of Peruvian and German students in close connection with the local population, and were guided by the teaching team and external experts from different disciplines. The experience of working in multidisciplinary teams enabled the students to gain an understanding of complex issues leading to integrated design solutions. Additionally, the communities living around the intervention areas were target groups for the site-specific development of the solutions, based on local knowledge, skills and materials, since the entire process included participatory design processes.

Parties Involved

The two summer schools were organised by the Institute of Landscape Planning and Ecology at the Architecture and Urban Planning Faculty, University of Stuttgart. Each summer school was the final phase of a semester-long design studio offered as part of the "International Year" module for fifth-semester bachelor's students of architecture at the University of Stuttgart.

The coordinating partner in Lima for the two summer schools was the Research Centre of Architecture and the City (CIAC), Department of Architecture, Pontificia Catholic University of Peru (PUCP). For the second summer school, the supporting academic partner in Germany was Ostfalia University of Applied Sciences.

Another supporting academic partner in Lima was the Research Centre for Wastewater Treatment and Hazardous Waste (CITRAR) at the Faculty of Environmental Engineering, National University of Engineering. The Department of Spatial Planning and Sustainable Development at the Agricultural Engineering Faculty (FIA) of the National Agricultural University La Molina (UNALM) joined the second summer school.

At both summer schools, there was close cooperation with the San Martin de Porres Municipality, which provided information on the sites with guided visits, working places, construction tools, and security for the duration of the fieldwork.

For the second summer school, the Colegio 2088 Republica Federal de Alemania, located in Chuquitanta, San Martin de Porres, Lima, and the Colegio 4021 Daniel Alcides Carrion,

located in Parque Porcino, Ventanilla, Callao, provided workspace and support with the involvement of children, teachers, parents, and other associations.

The Callao Regional Government, Lima Metropolitan Municipality Park Services Office (SER-PAR), Lima Regional Program and the Natural Resources and Environmental Office supported the summer school by offering guided tours of the project site and/or other project case studies.

The gallery Centro de la Imagen in Lima provided space and support for a two-week public exhibition of the second summer school results.

Subjects, Issues, and Contents

The task of the summer schools was to develop and implement low-cost, productive water-sensitive urban design solutions that are both functional and beautiful and contribute to a sustainable urban environment. Such solutions should limit the wasteful consumption of potable water and show new approaches to harvesting or saving water, purifying water, reusing nutrients for fertilisation or food production, and using local or recycled materials.

The aim was to develop strategic temporary interventions at the first summer school and semi-permanent installations at the second summer school in the form of design prototypes that would be tested for their viability with both experts and the community. The students were asked not to develop a master plan for the whole site, but rather to propose a minimal strategic intervention that could initiate a chain reaction of improvements. The final proposal had to possess the highest potential to be replicated in other open spaces in the future.

Methods, Scenarios, and Organisation

Each summer school was composed of two weeks of intensive exploration, design, and construction work, which mainly took place on-site and in close connection with the local community.

Participatory workshops were organised to establish a close connection between the students and the community. Having the community involved in the development of the project helped them to identify with the results of the summer school, and produced responsibilities

Fig. 9 Participatory design process led by professional social workers involving the students and the children and teachers from local schools [ILPÖ, 2012]

Fig. 10 Community members, local and international students working together in participatory design workshops [ILPÖ, 2012]

and commitment for future maintenance and further development of the implemented installations. Additionally, visits to related case study projects in Lima were organised.

The methodology for the summer school considered two main aspects. First, the students from different disciplines had to use their different individual competences and apply their different methods and tools; but all had to contribute to a joint project that integrated individual contributions. Second, the task of the workshop covered the whole process, from analyses to project implementation and a handing over to the community; as such, it was a quite complex task to be fulfilled within a short time.

To involve all disciplines equally in the process, the methodology of the summer schools combined five working phases and four different thematic missions. The working phases structured the process of project development and the missions made sure that the different important topics relating to the different disciplines were taken into account equally.

Fig. 11 Children were very actively involved in the development and implementation of ideas [ILPÖ, 2012].

Fig. 12 Students working together with community members and construction workers on the implementation of their project ideas [ILPÖ, 2013]

The five working phases were:
- Exploring (integrated context analysis)
- Programming (integrated needs analysis)
- Designing (integrated design proposal)
- Implementing (construction and management)
- Handing over (final event and future guidance).

The four thematic missions were:
- WATER/YAKU MISSION: Closing the urban water cycle
- PUBLIC SPACE/CANCHA MISSION: Attractive public space and social interaction
- EARTH/PACHA MISSION: Productive, water-sensitive and beautiful green
- PEOPLE/RUNA MISSION: Engaging with the local community.
  The selected names, Yaku, Cancha, Pacha and Runa, express the meaning of the missions in the local Quechua language.

Fig. 13 The built interventions demonstrated the natural process of water treatment and reuse to the local community. A constructed wetland was built for recycling greywater and promoting urban agriculture [ILPÖ, 2012].

Fig. 14 The task of the students was to organise a final event for demonstrating, celebrating and passing on the built experience to the community and local authorities [ILPÖ, 2013].

Instruments, Products, and Learning

The process and results of both summer schools were documented in the form of booklets, local and international exhibitions (eg. International Architecture Biennale Rotterdam 2014), and two videos in English and Spanish. Printed booklets were given to the local academic partners and the local administrations. All documentation was also made available online.

After each summer school, a public exhibition in Lima was organised and different academic and administrative institutions as well as the general public were invited.

Those activities proved effective at disseminating the water-sensitive urban design topic both at the academic level, resulting in follow-up activities, and at the local administration level, which resulted in a communication of the approach and ideas that were part of the ongoing LiWa research project activities.

Costs, Efforts, Resources, and Preparation

In the preparatory phase of each summer school, a group of German and Peruvian students took part in seminars and design studios on the topic of arid cities and water-sensitive urban design for one semester. At the same time, the German students attended Spanish courses. The teaching staff and researchers prepared the summer school programme in close cooperation with local partners and institutions. For the financing of the summer schools, proposals to different funding bodies (summer school 1: Sto Foundation; summer school 2: DAAD) had to be written and submitted. After the funding was acquired, there was an open call through email, the Internet, and Facebook for further participants from different disciplines to attend the summer schools. Based on an evaluation of their CVs, portfolios, and letters of motivation, the students were selected by a German-Peruvian selection committee. Before the start of the summer schools, between one and two weeks of intensive preparation in Lima was required as part of phase 3.

Each summer school was held for two weeks, with a budget of 10,000 euro (summer school 1) and 25,000 euro (summer school 2). The budget included costs of travel and accommodation, translation, participatory workshops, construction and documentation materials, documentation and exhibition design and implementation, and public relations. The teaching team from Germany consisted of university staff. The teaching and working space in Lima was provided by the local academic partners. In terms of local organisation, both summer schools were supported by the research project LiWa.

After the actual events of the two-week summer schools were over, there was a two-week intense working phase for the documentation of the workshop results, including layout, design, printing, and installation of the exhibition materials and coordination with the exhibition venue. The final production of the documentation took about three months, which mainly entailed translation and correction of the text in two languages. The preparation required support with layout and compilation of materials.

Essential Requirements

To run this type of summer school successfully and achieve sustainability of its results, it is essential to have committed staff in Germany and establish close cooperation with, and active involvement of, local partners—both the universities and the institutions operating in the area of work. As the time for conceptualising, designing, and implementing within a two-week summer school is very limited, it requires reliable support in terms of tool and material supply from the local partners and good practical and organisational skills on the part of the students.

As the didactic concept of the summer schools implied that much of the time was spent not in the "safe" university environment, but out in the field, a secure room at or close to the work-site for group meetings, plus basic hygienic facilities, are necessary.

Experiences

Summer schools as an extra academic activity can conflict with the schedule of the obligatory academic programme at the partner university, and some local students might not be able to participate on a regular basis during the whole summer school.

One possible recommendation is to aim to include the summer school in the academic curriculum of the partner university and provide credit points for participation. This could increase the level of commitment of the students and the support of the partner university.

Implementation

The design action oriented approach of the summer school was embedded in the structure of the research project and the process and results directly contribute to the research project activities. Additionally, some students from the summer school initiated further activities, did internships with the local project partners, and and continued developing their proposals after the end of the summer school.

Transfer and Dissemination Activities

Exhibitions of results, conferences, and interviews with local and international media, publishing documentation in printed form and online, establishing a blog and Facebook pages. Additionally, presentations by Peruvian summer school students were given at their own universities and institutes.

For more Information and Products

Find general information on the LiWa (Lima Water) research project at http://www.lima-water.de/index.html and on the Megacities Programme of the German federal Ministry of Education and Research (BMBF) at http://future-megacities.org

Some materials on the topic of water sensitive urban design of desert cities and the area of work, the Lower Chillón Watershed, and diploma thesis building up on the results of the summer schools are available for viewing:

- Atlas for the lower Chillon area: http://issuu.com/ilpoe/docs/atlas_lower_chillon

- Results of summer school 2012: http://issuu.com/ilpoe/docs/ilpe_lima_summerschool_complete

- Results of the summer school 2013: http://issuu.com/ilpoe/docs/booklet_summer_school_2013_-_issuu

- Results of the seminar "Cities out of water" 2012/13: http://issuu.com/ilpoe/docs/booklet_seminar_ws12-13_-_issuu

- Results of the International Design Studio 2012/13: http://issuu.com/ilpoe/docs/booklet_entwurf_ws12-13_-_issuu

- Results of the diploma thesis "Parque Lomas" (Marius Ege) 2012: http://issuu.com/marius.ege/docs/130207_booklet_parque_lomas_issuu

- Results of the diploma thesis "Integrated Open Space Strategies for Huaycán" (Andrea Ballestrini): http://issuu.com/andreabalestrini/docs/booklet_issuu

Video documentation from both summer schools can be viewed at http://vimeo.com/63071828 and http://vimeo.com/62033696.

Past, ongoing, and future activities can be followed at Blog Lower Chillón area at http://limabeyondthepark.wordpress.com/.

Facebook pages:

https://www.facebook.com/summerschoolbeyondthepark

https://www.facebook.com/pages/Beyond-the-Park_Rethinking-Landscapes/452636151455184

(All web links last checked on June 5th 2014)

References

Brugmans, G./Strien, J. (eds.) (2014): *IBABR - 2014 - Urban by Nature.* Catalogue of the International Architecture Biennale Rotterdam, p. 130

Brussel, M./Chambi, G. (eds.) (2008): *Atlas Ambiental de Lima.* Instituto Metropolitano de Planificación, Lima, Peru

Digesa, Ign, Imarpe, Imp, Inc, Indeci, Ingemmet, Inrena, Mem, Vivienda, Pett, San, Sedapal, and Senamhi (2008): *Atlas ambiental de Lima.* Lima

Eisenberg, B./Nemcova, E./Poblet, R./Stokman, A. (2012): "Hydro Urban Units—A Meso Scale Approach for Integrated Planning". In: *REAL CORP 2013: PLANNING TIMES, Acquario Romano (House of Architecture) conference,* Rome, Italy

Eisenberg, B./Nemcova, E./Poblet, R./Stokman, A. (2014): "Lima: a Megacity in the Desert"/"Lima: Lower Chillon River Plan"/"Lima: Integrated Urban Planning". In: Pahl-Weber, E./Schwartze, F. (Eds.): *Space Planning and Design. Integrated Planning and Design Solutions for Future Megacities.* Jovis Publishers, Berlin. pp. 27-34, 79-88, 139-165

Instituto Metropolitano de Planificacion (IMP) (2013): *Plan Regional Lima de Desarrollo Concentrado de Lima (2012-2015).* Lima

Instituto Nacional de Estadística e Informática (2012): *Estimaciones y Proyecciones de Población Total por Sexo de las Principales Ciudades 2000-2015.* https://docs.google.com/file/d/0B1WxBwWL6_X6cDZTbHN2TFctQjA/edit, 20.08.2013, Peru

Institute of Landscape Planning and Ecology (2012): *Valle bajo del Rio Chillón: Plan Marco de Desarrollo Paisajistico para el Valle Bajo del Rio Chillón, Hacia una Infraestructura Ecoligica, área de estudio del proyecto piloto de investigación LiWa.* Stuttgart

Kosow, H./León, C./Schütze, M. (2013): *Escenarios para el futuroy Callao 2040 Escenarios CIB, storylines & simulación LiWatool.* http://www.lima-water.de/documents/scenariobrochure.pdf, 11.12.2013

Ministry of Economy and Finance of Peru (2012): *Peru: Investment Climate, Economic and Social Outlook, October 2012*

Nemcova, E./Eisenberg, B./Poblet, R./Stokman, A. (2012): "Water Sensitive Design of Open Space Systems Ecological Infrastructure Strategy for Metropolitan Lima, Perú". In: *DNAI-Designing Nature as Infrastructure Conference. Technical University Munich*

Schütze, M. (2012): *Water and Wastewater Management in Megacities—How can a city prepare itself for the future? A project in Lima/Peru.* gwf-Wasser/Abwasser, S1/2012, pp. 64-8

Schwarz-v. Raumer, H.-G./Stokman, A. (2014): "Integrating Technology, Science and Creativity - a Challenge for collaborative Settings in Geodesign." In: Wissen Hayek, U./Fricker, P./Buhmann, E. (Eds.): *Peer Reviewed Proceedings of Digital Landscape Architecture 2014,* Wichmann Publishers, Berlin, pp. 15-26

Stokman, A. (2012): "Lima—Beyond the Park". In: *Topos 81 Water Landscapes.* pp. 102-9

Stokman A./Poblet R./Nemcova E. (2013): *International Summer School: Lima—Beyond the Park, Desert City, Culture and Infrastructure.* Institute of Landscape Planning and Ecology. University of Stuttgart

Stokman, A./Poblet, R./Nemcova, E. (2012): *International Summer School: Lima—Beyond the Park, coupling nature, culture and water infrastructure.* Institute of Landscape Planning and Ecology. University of Stuttgart

Notes

1 Instituto Nacional de Estadística e Informátic

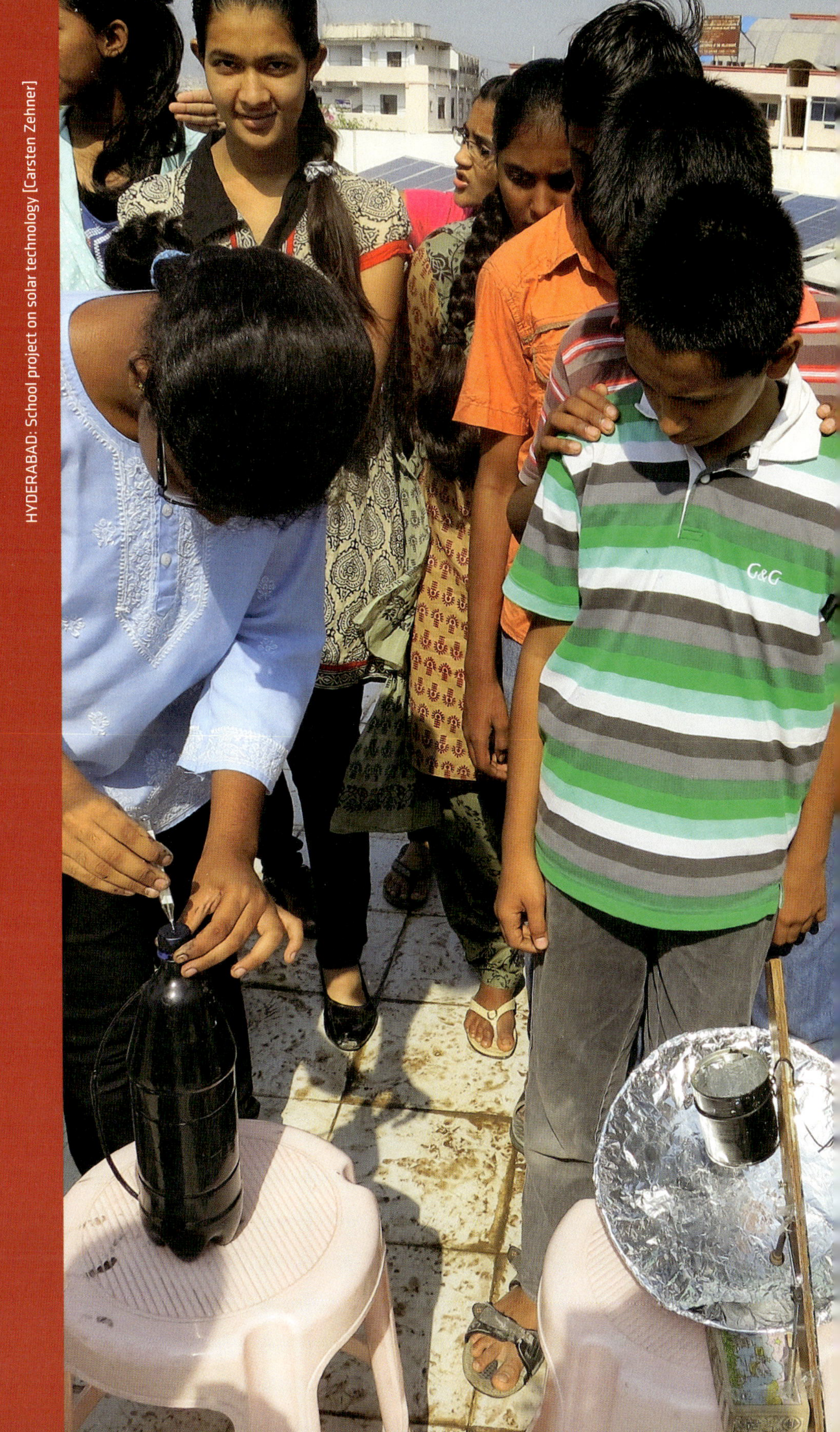

HYDERABAD: School project on solar technology [Carsten Zehner]

Lutz Meyer-Ohlendorf, Fritz Reusswig

Education for Sustainable Lifestyles—ESL

Keywords

Sustainability
Climate Change
Carbon Foot Printing
Emission Factor
Energy Audit
Carbon Cycle
Product Lifecycle
Waste management/Waste as a Resource
Climate Equity
Water Management
Organic Agriculture

Basic Information[1]

Location: India, Andhra Pradesh (AP), Emerging Megacity of Hyderabad
Ecology: Climate change is predicted to lead to extreme weather events, disastrous floods, heat waves, extreme droughts, and increasing water scarcity.
Population: (Hyderabad Metropolitan) 7,749,334, Population growth (decadal): India -17.64%; AP: 11.1% [Census of India 2011]. "Greater Hyderabad", a fast-growing metropolitan region in Southern India, will reach 10.5 million inhabitants by 2015.
Economy/Living Standard: Approximately one-third of the population lives below the poverty line and continues to suffer from severe food and health problems. The emerging megacity experiences rapid economic growth enabling higher living standards and modern lifestyles for the emerging middle class. This is, however, accompanied by escalating energy and resource consumption and constantly increasing greenhouse gas emissions per capita.
Governance: The core modules of analysis in the project follow the hypothesis that "getting the institutions right" is one main key to solve the problems of sustainable resource use in general and sustainable demands on climate and energy in particular. Whether or not a society will be able to cope with the impacts of climate change and increased scarcity of energy depends on its capacity to change human behaviour. This requires changing institutions, defined as "sets of rules" and governance structures, i.e., those "modes of organisation" that are necessary to put rules into practice.
Project focus: The project's main subjects are climate and energy in a complex transition process towards sustainable mitigation and adaptation strategies by changing institutions, governance structures, lifestyles, and consumption patterns in Hyderabad. Given the natural, social, and economic context of the emerging megacity, the question arises: what can be con-

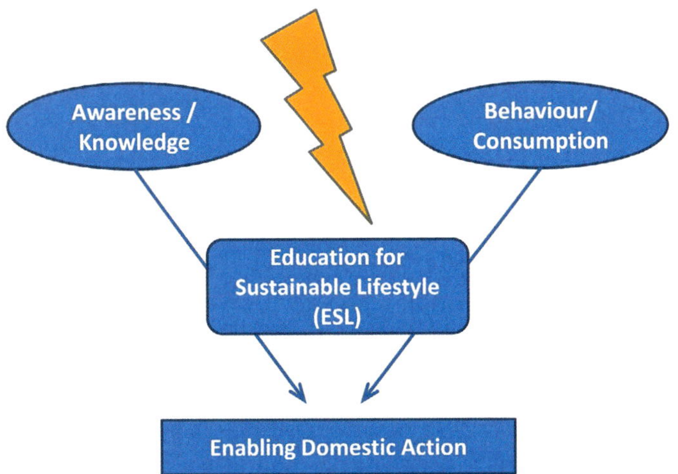

sidered a reasonable response to the anticipated climate change impact? This is the guiding research question of the project. In order to try and answer this question it was necessary to explore greenhouse gas mitigation, and adaptation strategies and ways towards increased energy efficiency and renewable energy.

Initial Situation

Urbanisation, economic development, and lifestyle changes will greatly increase the future greenhouse gas (GHG) emissions base in (urban) India, along with other environment-related problems [Satterthwaite 2009]. In order to tackle these challenges and channel social change towards sustainability, knowledge about global climate and environmental change and a broad understanding of sustainability are crucial. However, knowledge alone does not necessarily lead to behavioural change and action. Only direct translation of knowledge into action (learn, calculate, create, reduce, compete, communicate) will bridge the knowledge-behaviour gap [c.f. Mandl & Gerstenmaier 2000]. This means that learning sustainable lifestyles is a matter of active practical involvement and not of passive theoretical learning [Figure 1 ↗].

Background in the Field of Education

Today's schoolchildren are future decision-makers and are progressive enough to act as change agents in their school, family, neighbourhood, and city. While environmental issues do play a role in the curricula of India's school system, the way in which this is implemented lacks salience in terms of impact, didactic translation, and active engagement of the majority of teachers and students [Bharucha & Kumar 2002]. Given the structure and practice of the Indian school system today, a simple change of textbooks, as difficult as it would be, would not do the job. This is why the project Education for Sustainable Lifestyle (ESL) brings a new holistic environmental learning approach based on participation, flexibility and openness, creativity, peer-to-peer learning, and high levels of interaction between students, teachers, school management, and external stakeholders—for instance, parents, local businesses, people on the street. Moreover, the competitive character of the year-long intervention greatly adds to success in actively engaging the students and conveying enthusiasm for civic action.

Objectives and Targets

The aim of this project is to teach thinking on sustainability as an integrated life skill for students. The project encourages schoolchildren to internalise newly gained knowledge about the impacts of their personal behaviour/consumption (lifestyle) on the environment in general, and on climate in particular. Conceptually, the project focuses on climate change and climate impacts, but we deliberately put climate change in the broader context of sustainable urban development, not only to strengthen the project's impacts, but also to broaden the network of actors. The rather holistic character of the project also creates a link between curricular and environmental learning and social learning [Figures 2 and 3 ↗]. The involvement of the schools' neighbourhood is crucial here. Such an outreach is only achieved by encouraging students to conduct activities outside their schools, with or without the involvement of local stakeholders, such as community-based organisations, resident welfare associations, religious actors, and local businesses (local learning). This approach is very effective, as children in a team develop their own ideas and organise these activities themselves; they learn very practically, increase their interest and awareness outside the school premises, and gain practical insights into the complexity of human-environment interactions.

Students are encouraged to build a network with actors from the school's neighbouring community.

Target Groups

The project concept was specifically designed for schoolchildren aged thirteen to fourteen (eighth and ninth grades) in private and government schools in urban India. Indeed, ESL only targets students, but it aims to reach out much further by creating a motivated group of young people who will act as agents of change for sustainable lifestyle and consumption well beyond the school premises.

To assess existing knowledge, we conducted initial group discussions and encouraged the students to prepare short presentations on "any topic related to climate change" (one-week preparation time). With a few exceptions, the existing knowledge was very limited. Students were able to recite few—if any—concepts and were unable to connect them meaningfully, let alone link them to their own world. Moreover, it was striking to learn that in most cases, teachers tried to direct and convey the topic of climate change purely as a science subject, with humans playing only a small part. No reference was made, for example, to the vast transformation processes and associated environmental problems in and around the city of Hyderabad, or to the risks that climate change poses to the city. This first assessment during the initial phase of the project suggested that a great proportion of schoolchildren in urban India lack a genuine interest in, and understanding of, climate change and issues related to sustainability.

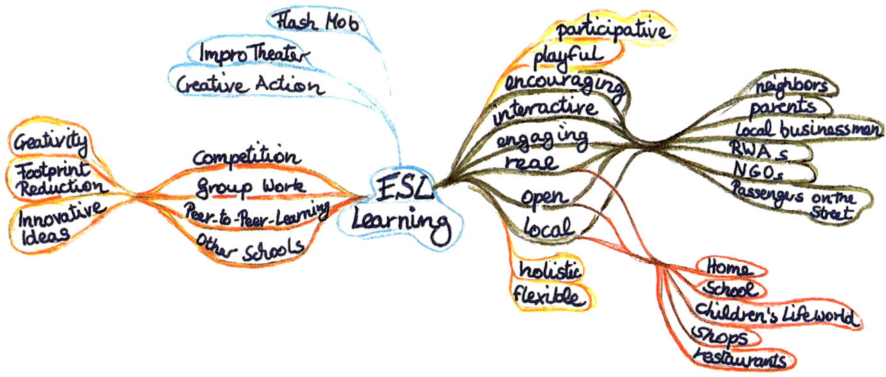

Fig. 3 Concepts taught during the Green Week [Authors]

Fig. 4 Drawing of a neighbourhood map: Students are encouraged to build a network with actors from the school's neighbouring community [Authors]

Parties Involved

The initial concept was developed by the team of researchers at the Potsdam Institute for Climate Impact Research[2] (PIK) on the basis of previously conducted research in Hyderabad. It was then further adapted and refined following several interactions with the direct project partners, no2co2, EcoSlate, and Nexus Institute, mostly via telephone conferences.

During the kick-off workshop in Hyderabad in October 2011, the concept was presented to the participating schools; the structure and schedule were discussed and final adjustments were made.

Some of the learning material and content were brought in by no2co2 and EcoSlate. Much of this was adapted to the specific learning conditions of the teachers' training and the situation in the different schools, in order to further develop the tools and material and optimise them for the rationale of the project.

The emission factor database for calculating carbon footprints was provided by no2co2, which developed the first India-specific web-based carbon calculator.[3]

Subjects, Issues, and Contents

Environmental education today already constitutes an integral part of the secondary education curriculum, but as shown above, it has not had the desired impacts. In order to address climate change and sustainability issues more meaningfully and practically, ESL emphasises the human dimension of these topics: consumption and lifestyle.

Methods, Scenarios, and Organisation

During the Green Week—a week-long, project-oriented learning module—students assess in a practical way the environmental impact of everyday practices in their school, neighbourhood, and home. Carbon foot printing, energy auditing, and transect walks are the practical tools at hand [Figures 5 and 6 ↗] . The underlying concepts behind the theoretical foundation of this practice-oriented learning approach were taught in a playful and interactive way using short animated films.

Instruments, Products, and Learning

ESL provides the school with a database of comprehensive learning material (collection of animated films, PowerPoint presentations, and printed material). It offers a tool kit for carbon footprint calculation with all the required emission factors, a web-based calculator from no2co2, and simple paper-based calculation sheets (material created by no2co2). ESL provides the tools for conducting an energy audit in the school with formulas, calculation sheets, and wattage of different appliances (material created by no2co2).

ESL, in collaboration with no2co2, has developed an energy minimisation calculator, which works online and calculates the savings of GHG emissions along with monetary savings obtained through technological improvements.

ESL has developed a manual, which explains the main concepts in very simple terms and offers a clear guideline for conducting ESL. It explains the tools and calculation sheets and encourages students and teachers to become active to achieve greater sustainability.

Experiences

The first pilot run of ESL had a limited reach, with only five schools involved. However, this small-scale target was critical in order to allow a very close and intensive exchange between the ESL team and the classroom. It helped us to get a sense of the level of understanding and the effects of teaching, and explore and experiment with new learning methods and applied tools. It allowed us to gain important insights into the methodology of learning for sustainable development and has contributed to developing new tools and techniques to involve students directly and holistically in the process of learning-by-doing.

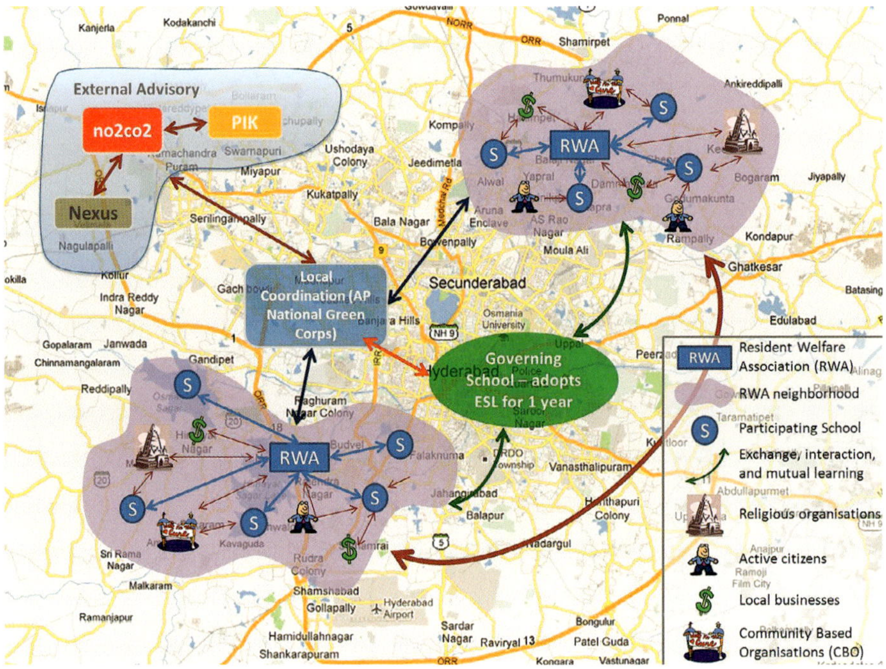

Fig. 7 Structure and involvement of the most important stakeholders of an upgraded ESL project aimed at the school neighbourhood [Authors]

For reasons of dissemination, however, we had to develop the structure of the ESL project further by maintaining flexibility—such as integrating as many different kinds of schools, socially-speaking, as possible—while also reducing external supervision to a minimum. With the upgraded version of ESL, we have developed a model that can easily be transferred to other cities; it works with very limited financial and human resources; and it emphasises a rather new component—the involvement of the school's neighbourhood.

Transfer and Dissemination Activities

With the upgraded version of ESL2, we are in the process of initiating a second pilot phase in Hyderabad in cooperation with the local partner no2co2. ESL2 is a more independent system in which an ESL qualified school—the "ESL Governing School" (tenth-grade students and selected teachers)—is involved in coordination and training, and supports the local coordinator. Through this new concept, ESL draws on its own resources, as the trained students and teachers rotate and bring their knowledge and experiences directly to the participating schools. This not only reduces the amount of external input, but it also greatly benefits the Governing Schools' students [Figure 7 ↗].

ESL2 emphasises to a greater extent than in the previous phase the link between the school and its surrounding community. The participating schools are encouraged to involve local community stakeholders, such as community-based organisations (CBOs), resident welfare associations (RWAs), local businesses, religious organisations (temple, church, and mosque), active citizens, and other participating schools. ESL2 gains a great deal from having outreach as one of its main components; one that is based on developing an active network of committed people and organisations around the participating schools willing to work together towards achieving sustainable development at the community level.

This adapted concept will be tested in a second pilot programme, and still requires scientific supervision in order to achieve its objectives. Therefore, its next pilot phase will be supervised and monitored by PIK and no2co2.

For more Information and Products

Find general information on the Sustainable Hyderabad project at
http://www.sustainable-hyderabad.de

All information regarding the Megacities programme of the German Federal Ministry of Education and Research is provided at
http://future-megacities.org/

Some of the materials, such as further documentation, concept, news coverage, and training material, will be offered for download at
http://www.sustainable-hyderabad.de

The first India-specific Carbon Calculator provided by our partner organisation no2co2 can be accessed at
http://www.no2co2.in/CarbonCalculator.php

The Minimize Energy Calculator developed by no2co2 and PIK can be accessed at
http://www.no2co2.in/login.php

For any further enquiries, please contact the authors.

References

Bharucha, E./Kumar, S. (2002): *Environmentalizing school curricula in India: Challenges and opportunities*. Manuscript

Mandl, H./Gerstenmaier, J. (2000): *Die Kluft zwischen Wissen und Handeln—Empirische und theoretische Lösungsansätze*. Hogrefe-Verlag, Göttingen

Satterthwaite, D. (2009): "The implications of population growth and urbanization for climate change". In: *Environment and Urbanization* Vol. 21 (No. 2), pp. 545–68

Notes

1 Written by Srinivasa Srigiri, Humboldt-Universität zu Berlin

2   Potsdam-Institut für Klimafolgenforschung

3 http://www.no2co2.in/

堡项目简介
Xingfu Road Passive House
构：
砖墙200mm+岩棉板300mm（导热系数=0.040w/mk），传热系数：0.14w/m²k
三玻塑料窗，low-E玻璃，传热系数：0.80w/m²k（德国进口产品）
楼板350mm+挤塑板400mm+覆土300mm；传热系数：0.10w/m²k
350mm+挤塑板300mm，传热系数0.16w/m²k
钢筋混凝土墙300mm，200mm，传热系数：0.15w/m²k
≤0.04w/m²k
幸福
一次性
建筑能
夏季制

总建筑
（地上
建筑体
建筑层
体
高
地下
地上
地上四

URUMQI: On-site exhibition about the first passive house [Bernd Mahrin]

Bernd Franke, Christian Hennecke, Berthold Kaufman, Xiaoyan Peng, Ming Liu

Training on the Way to the First Passive House in Western China

Keywords

> **Low-energy Buildings**
> **Passive House**
> **Energy Planning**
> **Architectural Design**
> **Quality Control**
> **Student Exchange**

Basic Information

Location: Urumqi, capital of the autonomous region of Xinjiang Uyghur in the north-west of the People's Republic of China. It is the largest city in China's western interior, located 3,600 km away from the nearest ocean—as far as no other city on earth.

Climate: Semi-arid climate with warm summers and very cold winters

Ecology: Urumqi is considered one of the most polluted cities in China and the world [Wikipedia 2014]. The 2020 heat energy consumption by the residential building stock added during the current decade will be comparable to Germany's greenhouse gas (GHG) emissions.

Population: 3.3 million people live in Urumqi. China is experiencing rapid demographic changes. The share of citizens living in urban environments will increase from about 36% in 2000 to around 56% in 2020.

Economy/Construction Volume: The economic development (GDP 2000/2020) and other drivers have led to an unprecedented building boom, which, as in the case of the Xinjiang Uyghur Autonomous Region is reinforced by the Chinese government's "Go West" policies. In China, new residential space is being constructed at a rate of 2 billion m^2 per year. In Xinjiang's capital Urumqi, construction reached 10 million m^2 in 2013, which is equivalent to half of all apartment construction in Germany. Under a business-as-usual scenario, the demand for energy for space heating in these new buildings will decline from 79 kWh/(m^2*year) in 2000 to 64 kWh/(m^2*year) by 2020 in northern climates (34% of the population).

Living Standard: Urumqi has developed economically and now serves as a regional transport node, cultural, and commercial centre [Wikipedia 2014]. Urban residents in China require and enjoy on average higher living standards than rural populations: the average surface living area of apartments has increased to 94 m^2, which is similar to industrialised countries, and the number of persons per apartment is decreasing.

Initial Situation

China, which is already the world's largest consumer of energy and emitter of greenhouse gases, established regulations and standards for building energy consumption, which have become stricter over the years. However, the energy consumption of new buildings is usually calculated only at the planning stage and not verified regularly. Actual energy performance therefore often falls short of achieving the legally stipulated standard. This situation threatens to undermine the planned reduction of Chinese GHG emissions by 40–45%, a voluntary commitment under the Copenhagen Accord. In addition, the best available technology and practice could allow space heating demand to be substantially reduced, to an amount below the current Chinese performance levels: *Passive Houses* consume only ≤ 15 kWh/(m²*year) in heating, while those labelled *Low Energy Buildings* require 50 kWh/(m²*year) or more.

Special Background

Sustainable energy supply and consumption in the housing sector is a great challenge in Urumqi, where cold winters—with an average temperature of -14.4°C in January—drive the demand for heating to a very high level of 5,000 heating degree days for a base temperature of 20°C. Due to low stack heights, a lack of adequate pollution control, and frequent inversions in the cold winter months, emissions from heat generation are a major cause of air pollution.

Several model projects to construct low-energy buildings and passive houses in particular have been implemented in China, with Urumqi as an example. However, these remain insular solutions with hitherto very limited replication. The knowledge and technologies for constructing low-energy housing are in principle available in China. However, architects, building planners, construction companies, and their staff lack experience in combining these technologies to create the complex system that a low-energy house represents: that is, matching equipment, construction materials, construction quality, adequate operation, and maintenance. Furthermore, existing technologies and techniques often need to be adapted to local customs. Tailored capacity building is therefore paramount to meet these challenges.

Objectives and Targets

The overall objective of the capacity development activities was to improve the energy efficiency of buildings by strengthening the long-term planning, including standard setting, of the City of Urumqi; by improving the sustainability of building design and the supply of adequate building components; by training construction personnel; and by offering adequate quality control. The lighthouse projects were designed as focal points to trigger the capacity development needs. In order to achieve a lasting impact, stakeholders in the public and private sector, including those in other cities of Xinjiang Province, were involved.

Target Groups, Parties Involved

The target groups, parties involved, and summary of project activities are listed below.

Fig. 2 Stakeholders and their roles

Target groups	Party	Activities
Policymakers	Xinjiang Department of Environment	Lecture on energy policy for senior staff, study tour in Germany
City planners	City of Urumqi Construction Committee	Three-month training of senior staff person in Germany in 2011, joint pilot projects
Architects and engineers	Xinjiang Institute of Architectural Design and Research	Development of Design Handbook, three-month training of senior staff person in Germany in 2011, joint pilot projects (retrofit and passive house)
Real estate developers	Dacheng International Co., Ltd.	Lighthouse project (passive house), feasibility study on passive house high-rise, study tour in Germany
Construction company staff	Happy World Co., Urumqi Gangyuan Architectural Decoration Engineering Co., Beijing	Lighthouse project (passive house), study tour in Germany by senior personnel
University teachers and students	University of Xinjiang, Faculty of Architecture	Development of design handbook, joint pilot projects
Building-component manufacturers	German and Chinese companies manufacturing windows, insulation materials, ventilation systems	Exchange to evaluate marketing opportunities and need for tailored products
Middle-school teachers and students	No. 8 Middle School, Urumqi	Student/teacher exchange, website development

Fig. 3   Energy retrofit of a training centre in Urumqi's Nanshan region: The city's first zero-CO_2-emissions building [Authors]

Fig. 4   The first passive house in Western China has multifunctional uses and reduces the heat energy demand by 85% compared to the existing standard [Culturebridge Architects].

Subjects, Issues, and Contents

Two lighthouse projects were conducted in order to demonstrate that a greater reduction in energy-demand in existing and newly constructed buildings can actually be achieved at reasonable costs.

Zero-emission retrofit: In the south of Urumqi, the agricultural education centre underwent an energy retrofit that transformed the building into the first zero CO_2-emission building in the provincial capital. Heating during the very cold winters is supplied by solar heating using innovative seasonal storage; the entire demand for electricity is met by a photovoltaic system. The demand for heating was reduced by more than 85%, all by optimising the building design, improving the insulation of walls and windows, and installing floor heating and a heat-recovery system. Starting in 2011, annual emissions of 88 tonnes of CO_2 are avoided. The local partners (Construction Committee of Urumqi, University of Xinjiang and the Xinjiang New Energy Institute) cooperated with the German partners IFEU Heidelberg, Culturebridge Architects, and the Passive House Institute. The energy certificate for the first zero-emission building in Urumqi provides a transparent picture of the improvements and serves as a role model for other projects. The demand for heating energy was reduced to a mere 50% of the recently adopted standard for new buildings. The renovation cost of about 2,500 RMB (270 euro) per m^2 was only partly energy related; experience gained in this project will help to tailor energy retrofit options to other buildings.

The first passive house in Western China: A passive house is a building in which a comfortable interior climate can be maintained with very low extra heating and cooling systems. The house is heated mainly by using heat sources in the building, such as lights, appliances, and the body temperature of residents—hence the term "passive". According to the Darmstadt/Germany Passive House Institute, the demand for heating should be lower than 15 kWh/m^2*a, with a total primary energy demand below 120 kWh/m^2*a relative to net usable area. To meet the challenging climate conditions, the first passive house is being constructed on Urumqi's Xingfu Lu (Happiness Rd.) by Dacheng Real Estate Co., a major investor in public and private buildings in Urumqi. The mixed-use building with a total floor space of 7,979 m^2 is designed to meet the passive house standard. The key components for maximising heat recovery are good insulation of the roof and walls [U-factor <0.15 W/(m^2*K], high-quality windows [U-factor of <0.8 W/(m^2*K)], a mechanical ventilation system with heat recovery (>75%) from exhaust air to supply air, and an airtight building (airflow of <0.6 h-1 during pressure test at 50 Pa). A passive house will have a demand for heating that is just 13% of that of houses built to the 2010 standard for new buildings in Urumqi. The Xingfubao passive house project has a sustainable building design that is attractive to clients despite its higher construction costs. It will demonstrate that a market for energy-efficient buildings can be created. The experience gained in this project is of great value to Urumqi and beyond.

Developing new standards: In 2014, Urumqi will adopt a new standard of 70-kWh/(m^2*a) gross surface area for new buildings. Standards for ultra-low-energy buildings, such as passive houses, are in preparation. Given the large volume of construction, the potential savings in energy demand and CO_2 emissions are substantial.

Methods, Scenarios, Organisation, Instruments, Products, and Learning

Workshops and conferences: During the course of the project, one international conference and nineteen thematic workshops were organised by the Sino-German team, ranging from an overview conference on energy and buildings to workshops on passive house design, and specialised topical workshops related to the lighthouse projects. In all cases, translating workshop materials into Chinese was an essential prerequisite for success.

Development of specific training materials: A 108-page design handbook, *Sustainable Elements for the Development for the Dryland Megacity Urumqi*, was developed. It focuses on the design of low-energy buildings adapted to cold winters and dry, hot summers. The design combined elements of traditional atrium buildings that could be adapted to the use of heated indoor spaces year-round. This was demonstrated by using designs of prototypes of different building sizes, types, and city regions (urban/suburban) and showing how theoretical approaches (A/V ratio, passive cooling, etc.) could be put into practice in a meaningful way—all while balancing ecological, economic, and social factors. The bilingual (English and Chinese) handbook was distributed via the project website, at conferences, and explained in detail during special lectures.

Passive house study tours: At the beginning of the project, there were no passive houses to visit in China. In order to gain a better understanding of the design principles and their

Fig. 5 Urumqi's first Sino-German workshop on energy efficiency set the stage during the project's prephase in January 2007 [Authors]

Fig. 6 Sustainable urban planning brochure for Urumqi [Authors]

practical application, visits to a large range of existing passive house sites were conducted. This triggered interest and strengthened motivation among the local stakeholders, including the local investor Dacheng International, to start the lighthouse project in Urumqi.

Support for three-month scholar visits: The BMBF allocated funding to senior experts from Urumqi to visit Germany for three months. This was particularly useful in allowing two experts—Ms. Peng Xiaoyan from the Urumqi City Construction Committee and Mr. Liu Ming from the Xinjiang Institute of Architectural Design and Research—to get a deeper understanding of policies, funding, technical issues, and quality control associated with building energy efficiency in Germany in general and in passive houses in particular. These two individuals are essential in guaranteeing support on the Chinese side.

Architect-to-architect exchange: The design of a passive house requires careful attention to detail. This includes the A/V ratio, passive solar gains, window design, thermal bridges, and ventilation system. Culturebridge Architects, the German architecture firm, was responsible for the general building design of the passive house in Urumqi, while the Xinjiang Institute of Architectural Design and Research prepared detailed drawings, taking into account general building standards in China. Many adjustments and iterations were necessary in the

collaboration between the two partners, such as reducing the number of thermal bridges by eliminating unnecessary support structures for façade mounting.

Practical construction-site training: Given the amount of ongoing construction in Urumqi (10 million m^2 per year) and the limited training that migrant construction workers obtain, quality control is a great challenge in general. The passive house requirements demand great attention to a number of details, such as the installation of 30-cm XPS insulation, the integration with façade design, airtightness of window seals, and ventilation-system design. This is being achieved in three steps: (a) capacity building at the Training Centre for Sustainable Construction in Cottbus, Germany; (b) a series of training workshops in Urumqi; and (c) air-tightness check with blower door testing following the installation of windows.

Implementation

The entire set of activities was designed to facilitate the completion of the two lighthouse projects.

A feasibility study was conducted together with Dacheng Co. for a 173-m-tall high-rise building, the Dacheng International Tower B, which would be the second-tallest building in Urumqi. Although this project is in its initial planning stages, the RECAST Urumqi team has analysed the possibility of building a true passive house with a heat energy demand of <15 kWh/(m^2*a) and a primary energy demand of <120 kWh/(m^2*a). The design includes 15-cm insulation on the external walls, passive-house windows, and a high-quality heat-recovery system. Simultaneously, the size of the window area and the external shading coefficient in summer need to be optimised in order to keep the demand for cooling as low as possible.

The long-term economic feasibility of high-quality, ultra-low-energy houses is considered by local investors and government officials to be high. Other extra-low-energy building projects in the Xinjiang cities of Karamay and Changji, currently in the planning phase, will build on the experience gained during the RECAST prototype projects. Information exchange with other projects—for example, an apartment complex in Qinhuangdao (Hebei Province), supported by the German Energy Agency (dena)—ensures that more and more passive houses will be built in China in the near future.

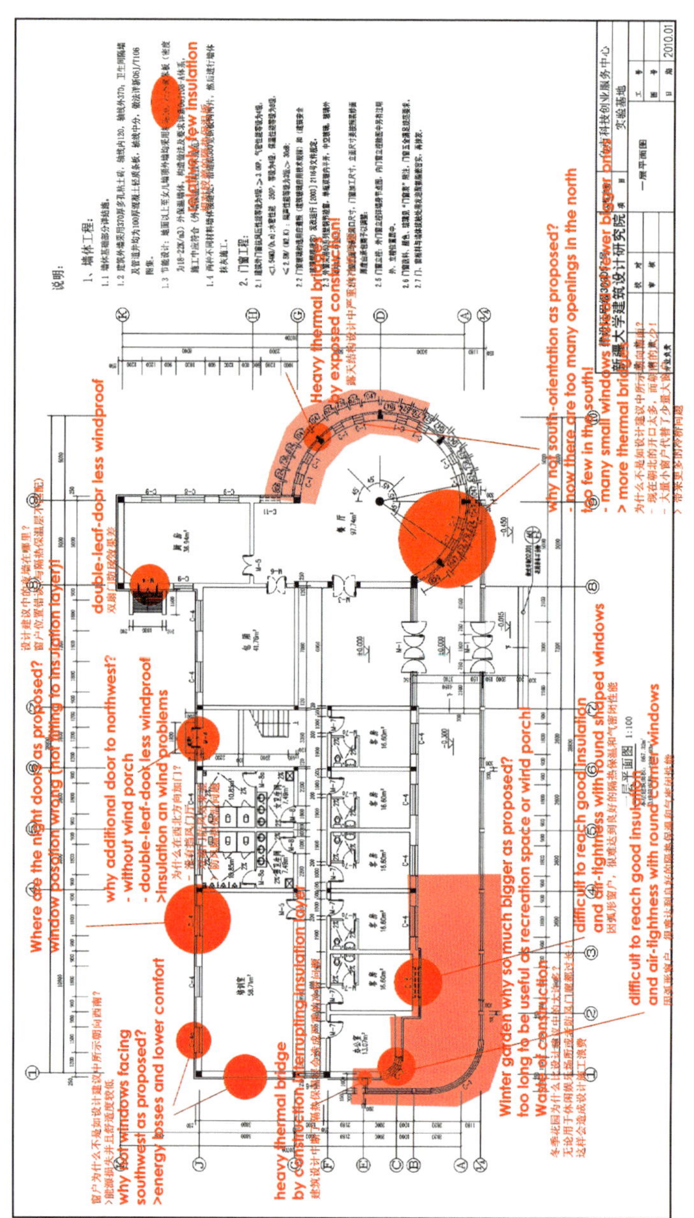
Where are the right door as proposed?
window position wrong (not going to insulation layer)!
double-leaf-door less windproof
why additional door to northwest?
- without wind porch
- double-leaf-door less windproof
>insulation an wind problems
Heavy thermal bridges by exposed construction!
relatively few insulation
why not south-orientation as proposed?
- now there are too many openings in the north
too few in the south!
- many small windows
> more thermal bridges
fewer bigger windows
difficult to reach good insulation
and air-tightness with round shaped windows
difficult to reach good insulation
and air-tightness with round corner windows
Winter garden why so much bigger as proposed?
too long to be useful as recreation space or wind porch
Waste of construction
heavy thermal bridge
by construction! interrupting insulation layer
why only windows facing
southwest as proposed?
>energy losses and lower comfort

Fig. 10   Training of senior construction personnel in Cottbus, November 2012 [Authors]

Fig. 11   German students meet their friends in Urumqi [Authors]

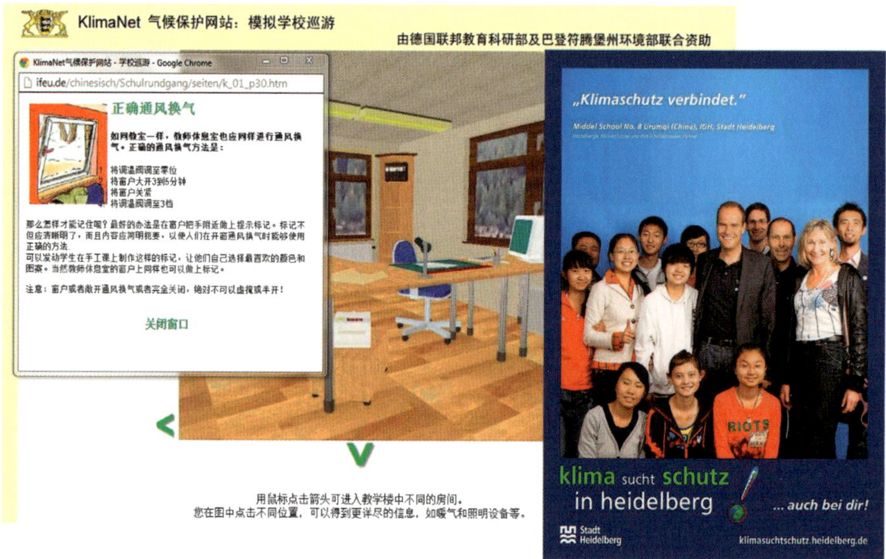

Fig. 13 In the Xinjiang city of Changji, many people turned up in January 2013 to learn about passive houses in Germany [Authors].

For more Information

Details on the projects and their implementation can be found in the "Task Group Energy" section of the project website: http://www.recast-urumqi.de/.

References

City of Urumqi Construction Committee (2012): *Report on the work on the demonstration projects for ultra-low power architecture applications in Urumqi (in Chinese)*. Urumqi

PHI Passivhaus-Institut (2010): *Guidelines for Implementing the Passive House Concept in the City and the Surroundings of Urumqi, Xinjiang, China*. Darmstadt

CAPACITY DEVELOPMENT THROUGH MEDIA AND COUNSELLING

HO CHI MINH CITY: The target building typology of the Handbook for Green Housing [Michael Waibel]

Michael Waibel

Trying to Persuade Rather than to Force People: The Approach of the Handbook for Green Housing

Keywords

Climate-adapted Housing
Energy-efficient Buildings
Green Housing
Holistic Approach
Bottom-up Approach
Multistakeholder Coalition
New Consumers
Ho Chi Minh City
Vietnam

Basic Information

Location: Ho Chi Minh City, Vietnam, north of the Mekong Delta.
Climate: The city is located in the tropical climate zone.
Population: Throughout the whole metropolitan area live slightly more than 10 million people.
Economy/Governance: Vietnam is an emerging economy, which is following a development path comparable to that of China. Since the mid-1980s, the country has gradually been introducing market-led reforms. The entry into the World Trade Organisation in 2007 can be considered a milestone of the economic transition. Overall, the reform process has been very successful. First and foremost poverty levels could be significantly reduced. Vietnam's big cities have been the engine of the reform process with Ho Chi Minh City, the country's first megacity, as economic spearhead. However, climate change seems to be endangering the tremendous progress Vietnam has achieved.

Initial Situation

During the course of transition, energy consumption has increased at almost double the speed of the astonishing economic growth. Buildings offer enormous potential for the reduction of greenhouse gas emissions and increasing energy consumption. This is particularly true in Vietnam, where the amount of construction activity is unprecedented. The final energy consumption within the residential sector is 54% of Vietnam's total. This proportion is very high and more than double then world average. Within the Megacity Research Project, TP. Ho Chi Minh—Integrative Urban and Environmental Planning Framework Adaptation to Climate

Fig. 1   Emerging skyline of Ho Chi Minh City, Vietnam [Author]

Fig. 2   Central Business District of Ho Chi Minh City, Vietnam [Author]

Change, a transdisciplinary team consisting of an architect from Darmstadt University, a construction engineer from Stuttgart University, the company, EnergyDesign Asia, as well as a social scientist from Hamburg University aim to promote climate-adapted housing and energy-efficient buildings in Vietnam.

Special Background

In Vietnam, modern, glass and steel architecture is preferred to traditional "tropical" architecture. Despite the enormous architectural heritage in terms of bioclimatic design, until the nineteen-seventies, Vietnam seems to have lost a part of its know-how in terms of design and construction concerning energy-efficient buildings. New buildings are equipped with energy-intensive A/C technology. The rapidly emerging urban middle-class population, the so-called new consumers, have increasingly resource-intensive lifestyles. New values are formed along with new life concepts, where new aspirations and possibilities are established. The danger is that issues of sustainability and long-term benefit that are crucial for society and humankind are neglected when making decisions about how to define the new status sought after.

Our analysis showed that most energy within a residential building is spent on cooling, followed by energy needed for heating water. The most important reasons for losing cooling energy are insufficient insulation of the walls and low-quality windows. Our surveys verified that the amount of living space (36 m^2/capita) and the amount of electricity consumption (340 kWh/month/capita) among the urban middle-class population in HCMC is almost the same as in Germany. Only a few households (16%) provide (thermal) solar water heaters.

Fig. 3   Neighbourhood of the "New Consumers" in Vietnam [Ceyhan Cüce 2011]

Fig. 5   Front cover of the *Handbook for Green Housing*, Vietnamese Edition [Author]

SỔ TAY NGÔI NHÀ XANH
GIẢI PHÁP THÍCH ỨNG KHÍ HẬU VÀ TIẾT KIỆM NĂNG LƯỢNG CHO CÔNG TRÌNH TẠI THÀNH PHỐ HỒ CHÍ MINH
TIẾT KIỆM NĂNG LƯỢNG.
TIẾT KIỆM TIỀN!
PHIÊN BẢN 1: NHÀ PHỐ
NHÀ XUẤT BẢN GIAO THÔNG VẬN TẢI
được tài trợ bởi
VNEEP
EUROCHAM

Achieving more energy-efficient structures remains a tremendous challenge. Official regulations, like the Vietnamese energy-efficiency building code, are largely ignored. Furthermore, state representatives are not currently leading by example. Sectorial approaches dominate, whereas more horizontal cooperation is needed. Civil society organisations act in a rather isolated fashion. A balanced set of economic incentives to promote energy efficiency does not yet exist. Briefly, successful policies towards more sustainability need to be less top-down, more holistic, and more inclusive. Against this complex background, our transdisciplinary team decided to develop a handbook by a broad, multistakeholder coalition to increase ownership and dissemination.

Objectives and Targets

The main objective of the publication and dissemination of the *Handbook for Green Housing* is to maximise the enormous potential that the housing sector has for the reduction of greenhouse gas emissions in Vietnam. Thus, a bottom-up approach is being followed, by trying to convince people rather than to coerce them—for example, by top-down regulations. In general, the *Handbook for Green Housing* pursues a holistic approach: the range of principles and measures introduced covers all construction and design aspects of buildings, as well the behavioural dimension. This includes information on how to rediscover the basic principles of bioclimatic architecture.

Target Groups

The main target group of the *Handbook for Green Housing* are homebuilders among the rapidly emerging urban middle-class population, the so-called new consumers. They will be persuaded by informing them about short payback times regarding the implementation of measures in the field of climate-adapted housing and energy-efficient buildings. In this context, the slogan "Save Energy, Save Money" was printed on the front cover of the handbook. However, the *Handbook for Green Housing* also offers valuable advice and inspiration for small and medium-sized construction companies from the construction and building sector, developer companies, higher education institutions, and local administration.

Parties Involved

During the development and production process of the *Handbook for Green Housing*, the aim was to create multistakeholder coalitions with representatives from government, the corporate sector, and from civil society. This was undertaken to increase local ownership, to reflect the comprehensive nature of this product, and to overcome institutional fragmentation prevalent in Vietnam. For example, contributions to the book were submitted by representatives from the Department of Construction of Ho Chi Minh City, from the Ministry of Science and Technology of Vietnam, the University of Architecture of Ho Chi Minh City, and from a local NGO, Live & Learn.

Subjects, Issues, and Contents

The *Handbook for Green Housing* is a tangible output introducing a comprehensive set of principles and measures by means of an easy-to-understand layout, to make the best of natural phenomena, like the sun and wind, as well as to limit natural disadvantages. The range of principles and measures introduced covers all construction and design aspects of buildings, as well the behavioural dimension. As a reference example, the most popular housing typology in urban Vietnam has been selected: the townhouse (*nhà phô*). In general, the principles and measures introduced should be understood like a menu from which homeowners choose

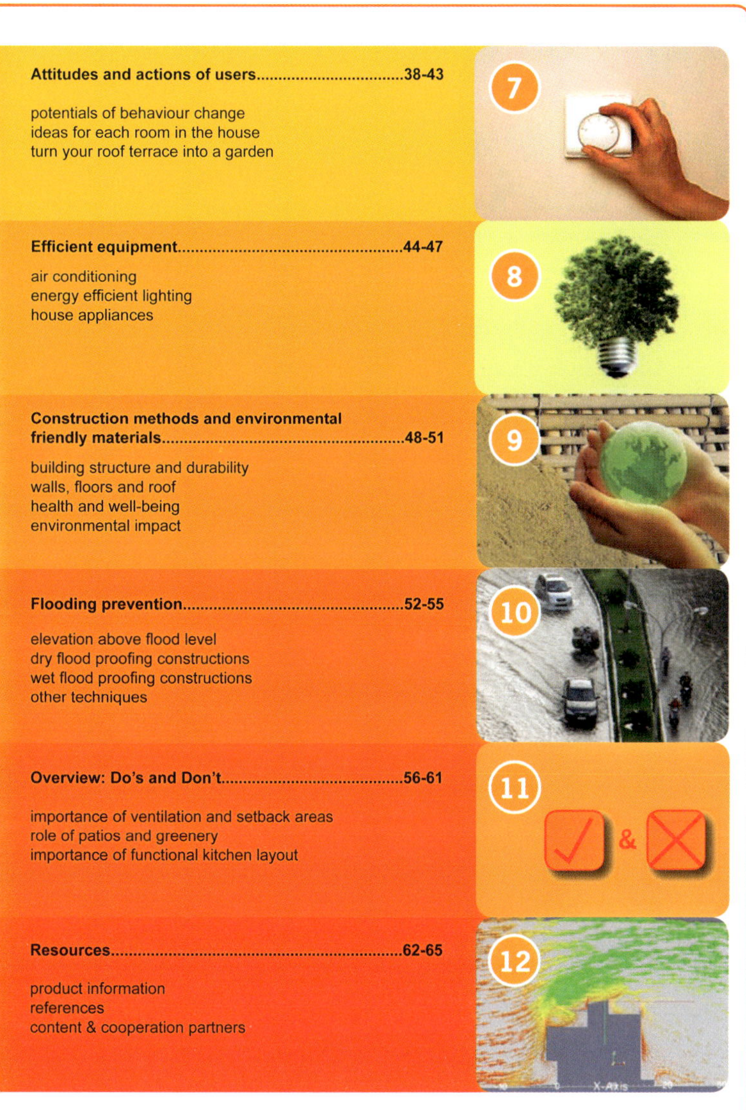

according to the individual capacities, needs, and personal preferences. Many of the ideas proposed do not cost anything, but offer multiple—individual and common—benefits.

Methods, Scenarios, and Organisation

The development and dissemination has been undertaken by a multistakeholder coalition. *The Handbook for Green Housing* has been officially endorsed by the national Ministry of Construction in Hanoi, the Department of Construction of Ho Chi Minh City, and the Vietnam National Energy Efficiency Programme (VNEEP) managed by the national Ministry of Trade and Industry.

Instruments, Products, and Learning

The final outcome is a tangible product: *Handbook for Green Housing*.

Costs, Efforts, Resources, and Preparation

The entire development process of the *Handbook for Green Housing* extended over a period of about two years. The inclusion of many stakeholders in Vietnam was time-consuming, but also rewarding. To secure high content quality, a lot of communication between the involved parties and numerous review meetings were needed. The European Chamber of Commerce in Vietnam (EuroCham), the Department of Construction of Ho Chi Minh City municipal government, and the Vietnam National Energy Efficiency Programme (VNEEP) generously contributed to the printing costs of the publication. The total circulation number of the printed Vietnamese edition was 5,000. Soft copies of the *Handbook for Green Housing* have been made available to read on numerous websites in Vietnam and internationally. This impressively illustrates the considerable commitment of the local stakeholders.

Essential Requirements

To establish a multistakeholder coalition regarding the development and dissemination process requires a lot of communication and the building of trust. Particularly for the scientists involved, it is very important to realise that the work is not completed after the publication of the handbook, but that impact can only be reached by means of an intensive dissemination campaign driven my multiple stakeholders. In a best-case scenario, the local stakeholders continue the dissemination efforts even after the termination of the project funding from Germany.

Experience

Remaining challenges:
- To get more local stakeholders on-board and to make the *Handbook for Green Housing* a local tool for sustainable building practice by overcoming the (false) expectations that foreign input might not fit the local demand and context.
- The identification of immediate connections between the increased erection of climate-adapted and energy-efficient buildings in Vietnam and the successful dissemination process of the *Handbook for Green Housing*.
- The acquisition of external financial resources regarding the further dissemination of the *Handbook for Green Housing*—for example, mailing activities, capacity building training, promotional tours around Vietnam, the organisation of media response, and advertisement (TV-spots), etc.

Implementation

The Megacity Research Project TP. Ho Chi Minh aims to develop a toolkit of measures for climate change adaptation and mitigation labelled the "Green Agenda". It contains different spatial levels of implementation, the urban scale, the neighbourhood scale, and the building

Fig. 7 Typical housing in Ho Chi Minh City [Author]

Fig. 8 Examples for the design layout [Author]

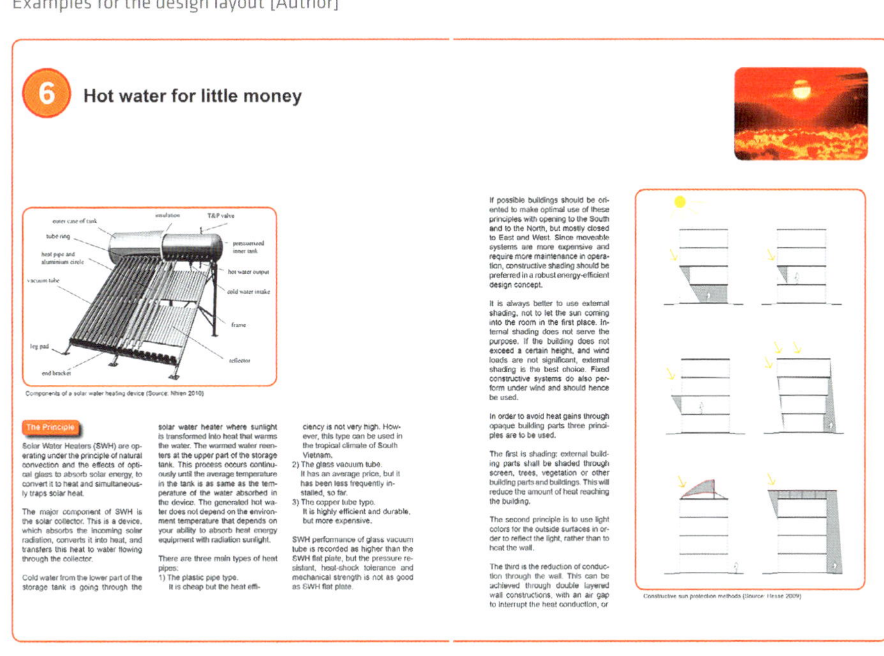

level. Within the framework of the Green Agenda, the main objective of the *Handbook for Green Housing* is to maximise the enormous potential the housing sector has for the reduction of greenhouse gas emissions in Vietnam. In this way, the development and dissemination of the Handbook for Green Housing, as well as of the second edition, the *Handbook for Green Products* are key elements of the work package, "Climate-Adapted Housing and Energy-Efficient Buildings in Vietnam" of the Megacity Research Project TP. Ho Chi Minh City.

Transfer and Dissemination Activities

- Presentations and Distribution at Conferences
- Representation at Fairs (Hanover Fair 2012, GreenBiz Vietnam 2013)
- Distribution to all Energy Efficiency Conservation Centres (EEC) in Vietnam and to all relevant libraries and to key decision-makers managed by VNEEP (Ministry of Trade and Industry)
- Selling of the *Handbook for Green Housing* at bookshops and online in Vietnam managed by the Publishing House (Transport Publishing House, Hanoi)
- Distribution to all district and sub-district government authorities in Ho Chi Minh City managed by the Department of Construction of HCMC municipal government (DoC, Ho Chi Minh City)
- Incorporation of the contents of the *Handbook for Green Housing* into the curriculum of Ho Chi Minh City University Department of Architecture and in other institutions of higher education
- Development of a second edition of the handbook the Handbook for Green Products, based on the same successful approach
- The *Handbook for Green Products* follows a dual strategy: 1) to give Vietnamese SME a platform to disseminate information about their innovative products and services 2) to inform home builders, construction companies, developer enterprises, and higher education institutions about general principles of how to make buildings more climate-adapted and energy-efficient by green housing products and services. The second edition was published in June 2013.

For more Information and Products

Web-Site of Megacity Research Project TP. Ho Chi Minh City: www.megacity-hcmc.org/

Download URL of the soft-copy of the English Edition of the Handbook for Green Housing: http://www-docs. tu-cottbus.de/megacity-hcmc/public/04_Publications/2011_edition_Handbook_for_Green_Housing_ENG.pdf

Download URL of the soft-copy of the Vietnamese Edition of the Handbook for Green Housing: http://www-docs. tu-cottbus.de/megacity-hcmc/public/04_Publications/2011_edition_Handbook_for_Green_Housing_VN.pdf

QR-Code for Download of English Edition

QR-Code for Download of Vietnamese Edition

References

Hesse, C./Schwede, D./Waibel, M. (biên tập) (2011): *Sổ tay ngôi nhà xanh: Giải pháp thích ứng khí hậu và tiết kiệm năng lượng cho công trình tại thành phố Hồ Chí Minh*. Phiên bản 1: Nhà phố. Hà Nội, Việt Nam; NXB Giao Thông Vận Tải, TP. 68 trang. ISBN 978-604-76-0030

Hesse, C./Schwede D./Waibel, M. (eds.) (2011): *Handbook for Green Housing: Climate-Adapted and Energy-Efficient Building Solutions for Ho Chi Minh City*. Edition 1: Town Houses. Hanoi, Vietnam: Transport Publishing House, 68 pages. ISBN 978-604-76-0031

Waibel, M. (ed.) (2013): *Handbook for Green Products: High-Quality Company Solutions towards Climate-Adapted Housing and Energy-Efficient Buildings in Vietnam*. Edition 2: Technical Constructive Green Housing Products and Green Services. Hanoi, Vietnam: Transport Publishing House, 72 pages. ISBN 978-604-76-0054-0

Waibel, M. (biên tập) (2013): *Sổ tay sản phẩm xanh: Giải pháp tối ưu của các doanh nghiệp nhằm thích ứng khí hậu và công trình sử dụng năng lượng hiệu quả ở Việt Nam*. Phiên bản 2: sản phẩm kĩ thuật-xây dựng cho ngôi nhà xanh và dịch vụ xanh. Nhà xuất bản Giao thông vận tải, Hà Nội /Việt Nam. 72 trang. ISBN 978-604-76-0060-0.

CASABLANCA: Ideas of urban agriculture have been supported by training courses in informal settlements [Lukas Born]

Gisela Prystav, Frank Helten

Urban Agriculture in Casablanca—Overview of the Capacity Development Approaches

Keywords

Urban Agriculture
Multifunctional Spatial Development
Planning
Awareness Raising
Training
Education
Income Generation
Food Security
Casablanca

Basic Information

Location: Casablanca, Morocco
Climate: Casablanca has a mild Mediterranean climate. Due to Atlantic Ocean's influence, there is little temperature variation and rarely extreme conditions.
Population: The Casablanca region is the largest urbanised region in the kingdom of Morocco, with 3.6 million inhabitants (2003) and an estimated population of 4.6 million inhabitants in 2015. 22% of the national urban population lives in Casablanca and 40% of the population is younger than 20 years old (1994).
Economy: Casablanca has become an economic and financial centre. It has one of the largest harbours in Africa and 60% of Moroccan industry is concentrated in this agglomeration (leather, textiles, mechanics, food, and chemical industries). Further industrial zones are also being created. Agriculture is of minor importance as an economic factor and an income source. The share of agriculture in Morocco's GDP is 11%, but only 1.6% originates from the Casablanca region. The most common crops in the area are cereals, which make up 80% of farmlands in Greater Casablanca's agricultural lands. Vegetable crops (tomatoes, potatoes, onions, carrots, etc.) and fodder crops are also grown. There is high pressure of speculation from the real estate sector on agricultural land.

Initial Situation

The scope of the project, Urban Agriculture as an Integrated Factor of Climate-Optimised Urban Development, Casablanca (UAC) included the urban region of greater Casablanca. The

Fig. 1   Densely built-up city and littering in public open spaces [Authors]

Fig. 2   Primary research dimensions [Authors]

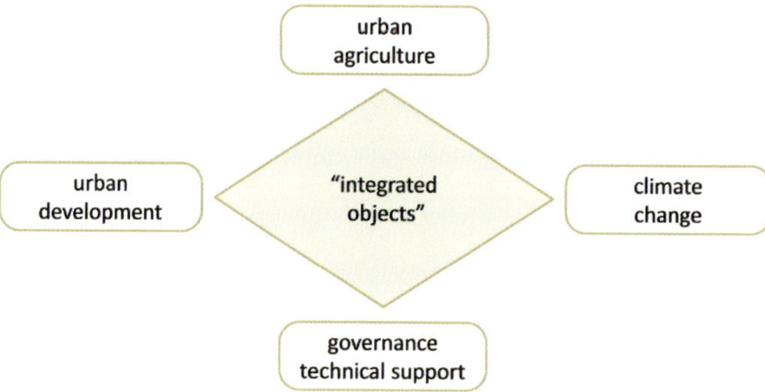

urban
agriculture
urban
development
"integrated
objects"
climate
change
governance
technical support

Fig. 3   New housing projects on the outskirts of Ouled Ahmed [Authors]

project studied whether, and how, agriculture can be integrated into the urban structure and the urban development process. Moreover, the project aimed at the design and implementation of solutions, which could contribute to sustainable and climate-optimised urban development in the sense of a multifunctional infrastructure. Additional questions addressed were: to what extent is Urban Agriculture (UA) an innovative strategy for the sustainable land conservation of urban open space, and to what extent, and how, can it contribute to the fight against poverty? The project was conceived as a transdisciplinary research effort, and thus involved various scientific disciplines and social actors from science and administration, civil society, and local citizens. It followed an action research approach combining bottom-up and top-down activities on the micro-, meso-, and macro-scale, and interlinks results on the different scales.

Background in the Fields of Planning and Implementation

Subsidiary production and subsistence gardening are rare in peri-urban areas and almost non-existent in the inner city. Farming has a low status and only generates small amounts of revenue. The peri-urban region is increasingly shaped by expanding neo-industrialisation and residential activities, creating pressure on neighbouring landowners and farmers, while informal settlements are spreading without official supervision close to these areas. Many previously rural communities—such as Dar Bouazza, Médiouna, Til Mellil, Sidi Maarouf, Lisasfa, Ain Harrouda, and Bouskoura—have been affected by the transformation of agricultural areas. Water is a rare and a threatened resource and the water table is dropping dramatically. The National Sewage Plan PNALE (Plan National d'Assainissement Liquide et d'Epuration) from 2005 aims at the treatment of all wastewater in Morocco until 2030, and the establishment of wastewater recovery. Nevertheless, thus far only three wastewater treatment plants are in operation currently in the peri-urban of Casablanca since 2012. A clear regulation for wastewater reuse in agriculture does not yet exist.

Objectives, Target Groups, and Parties Involved

The CD Measures' aims on different scales (micro, meso, and macro) and corresponding target groups
1. **Planning and participatory goal setting:** power planning, design competition, summer school, scenario workshop
   The objective is the joint investigation of the spatial situation regarding urban agriculture and development of potentials in terms of sustainable, climate-optimised urban development.
   Target groups: planning experts in administration and science, students; the scenario workshop and the integrated design competition involved disciplines and stakeholder levels in an interdisciplinary and transdisciplinary work process, in order to develop shared objectives and options.
2. **Awareness raising and topic setting:** eleven round-table discussions, two campaigns "Vision Verte Casablanca" with exhibitions, discussions, and pilot project events
   The objective is the dissemination of the issues among the experts and the public. The round-table discussions of specific aspects among government and academic experts. Topics include "Climate Change and Risk Management in the Casablanca Periphery",

Fig. 4   Architectural competition Ouled Ahmed 2010–Participants at work [Authors]

Fig. 5   La Coupole in Casablanca's Parc de la Ligue Arabe, location of the activities of Vision Verte II in 2011 [Authors]

Fig. 6   Round Table in Casablanca (La Coupole) [Authors]

Fig. 7   Women in Ouled Ahmed taking a break while cultivating the Solidarity Farm [Authors]

"Informality or UA in the new urban policy of the city in Morocco". The two month-long campaigns "Vision Verte Casablanca" in 2009 and 2011 aimed at publicising the project, including media reports on television, radio, and the daily press.

Target groups: experts (round-table discussions) and broader public (Vision Verte); active involvement and compliance of the project partners

3. **Enhancement of scientific expert knowledge:** joint studies on social practices, climate, water technology, agriculture related to UA; two study visits to Germany

4. **Technology exchange and technology implementation:** technical implementation and joint investigation particularly on high- and low-tech water treatment technologies

   Target groups three and four: Moroccan and German scientists (mutual learning!)

5. **Formation, training, and education:** farmer training, pedagogical farm, training for local women, school garden, e-Learning for children. Practical education; basic knowledge about the cultivation of vegetables, seed production, organic farming, processing and refinement of products, marketing and sale strategies

   Target groups: small and part-time farmers, local population, particularly women and schoolchildren

6. **Community building and communication:** self-organisation of farmers, traders, and women, establishment of associations. Forming education and training structures for communication and activities. Through the formation of associations, other options for further communication and joint activities were established.

   Target groups: small and part-time farmers, local population

Production of transformation knowledge: As a result of the CD activities and experience gathered during the CD process, it was possible to make a substantiated contribution as regards the production of transformation knowledge, proposed and laid down in the project's Action Plan.

Subjects, Issues, and Contents

The main approach is related to action research. On the micro-scale, four pilot projects constitute a laboratory to experiment, and test solutions on a small-scale to draw conclusions for the overall region. These are locations representing a specific combination of megacity challenges with urban agriculture.

- **Pilot Project 1–Industry and UA**
  Treatment and reuse of industrial wastewater for irrigation purposes
- **Pilot Project 2–Informal settlement and UA**
  Reintegration of UA for subsidiary provision and/or generating additional income for the local population, particularly women; implementation of, and training in establishing a school garden, a community garden tended by women, and a constructed wetland as low-tech water treatment application for irrigation
- **Pilot Project 3–Recreation and local tourism and UA**
  Training to foster the processing of local products and street markets for peri-urban tourists
- **Pilot Project 4–Healthy food production and UA**
  Building up skills for farmers in organic farming and creating direct sale structures with urban consumers

All CD activities are related to urban agriculture in the context of climate-optimised urban development, sustainable water management, social and economic coherence. The research results and findings from the pilot projects are projected to spatial structures and interlinked with spatial planning, design, implementation, and awareness raising.

Methods, Scenarios, and Organisation

Capacity building is an inherent element of various measures and used tools such as
- Scenario Workshop, Power Planning, Design competition, Summer School
- Eleven round-table discussions, two public campaigns Vision Verte Casablanca with exhibitions, discussions, and pilot project events

Fig. 9   Packing food baskets [Authors]

Fig. 10   Moroccan experts' field trip to Germany [Authors]

Fig. 11   Presenting results of the architectural competition [Authors]

- Joint studies
- Two study visits for scientific and administrative experts to Germany
- Implementation of high- and low-tech water treatment technologies
- Pedagogical farm, trainings for farmers
- Community garden, trainings for illiterate local women
- School garden, e Learning for children
- Self-organisation of farmers, traders and women, establishment of associations

Experience

The transdisciplinary project approach integrated actors from different social spheres—such as universities, administration, and civil society—in a collaborative work process, and was the major experience gained by the project. This process was perceived as a new and inspiring experience by the Moroccan partners. Regarding the pilot projects, the participatory approach of joint development and integrating the local population was of great importance to start a local dynamic and to foster the longevity of projects. The CD measures in the pilot projects not only enhanced knowledge on urban agriculture, but encouraged people to engage in other activities—including language courses, formation of associations—and strengthened the social network among them. Gardening did not stay in the limits of the pilot project land, but expanded into neighbouring gardens. The high rate of illiteracy and lack of experience hindered the training, and has to be recognised as a major obstacle in the extension of gardening activities from subsidiary production to income-generating commercialisation.

Transfer and Dissemination Activities

Urban agriculture is new and, thus far, fairly established in Casablanca as in most of the greater urban conglomerations. For this reason, capacity development is an important element of transfer and dissemination. There are local players who would like to continue the activities of the pilot project, as well as institutional actors who would like to foster urban agriculture. For the long-term success and dissemination of the concept of urban agriculture, local actors need institutional support on the local, regional, and national levels. The pilot project in the semi-informal settlement Ouled Ahmed is one of the Lighthouse Projects described in the proposal for an action plan. It is intended to continue and expand urban agriculture in the village in several ways, and to set up a showcase for urban agriculture in (semi-)informal settlements with particular regard on micro gardening. This includes the establishment of school gardens and the offer of training sessions. A training centre on urban agriculture, organised as a social enterprise, is one of the core elements of the action plan. The formation of a "water group"—which focuses on the reuse of water for irrigation with members from science, administration, and water supply—is another follow-up activity including capacity development elements. CD for young scientists and experts has been established as a result of the project in several scientific institutions and disciplines. This primarily includes the integration into the curriculum in the form of courses and practical training courses in the fields of planning and water technology.

For more Information and Products

Please visit the UAC Project Homepage www.uac-m.org and http://www.uac-m.org/publications/

References

Giseke, U. (2011): "Urban Agriculture Casablanca—Design as an Integrative Factor of Research". In: *Topos (The International Review of Landscape Architecture and Urban Design)* issue 74, ISBN: 978-3-7667-1896-9, research documentation from the Technische Universität Berlin (TUB)

Giseke, U. (Ed.) (2014): *Urban Agriculture for Growing City Regions—Connecting Urban-Rural Spheres in Casablanca*. London. To be published on 6 August 2014 by Routledge. http://www.routledge.com/books/details/9780415825016/

Helten, F.(2008): "Casablanca 20: A Laboratory for Rurbanism". In: *Megacities 10*, 107-116, Congress Proceedings, Faculty of Architecture, Delft University of Architecture

Helten, F. & Ouchker, J. (2010): "Grand Casablanca. Des approches et des actions innovatrices pour ledéveloppement juste et durable de la mégapole marocaine de demain." In: Sedjari, A. (Ed.) (2010): *Performance urbaine et droit à la ville*, 253-268, L'Harmattan

TEHRAN-KARAJ: The climate of the mountains affects the city [Lukas Born]

Ines Langer

Meteorological Measurements

Keywords

Mobile Measurements
Short Courses
Workshop
Meteorological Tower
Global, Diffuse, and Direct Radiation
Temperature
Relative Humidity
Wind Speed
Wind Direction

Basic Information

Location: Islamic Republic of Iran, Tehran-Karaj Region/Hashtgerd New Town

Climate: The climate in the Tehran-Karaj region is semi-arid.

Geomorphology: The region is heavily endangered by earthquakes.

Ecology: The population's awareness about energy and environment has not yet achieved a desirable level. As result, any efforts have to be supported by education and awareness-raising measures.

Population: Iran's population rose from 67 million inhabitants in 2003 to 80 million today. Of these, 15 million live in the Tehran-Karaj region and 50,000 in Hashtgerd. More than two-thirds of the Iranian people are under the age of thirty.

Education: The literacy rate is 82%. Women compose more than half of the university students. The general education system has improved enormously during the last three decades. Vocational training is strongly focused on academic knowledge and theoretical issues, whilst practical training is commonly disregarded.

Employment: According to official figures, the number of unemployed fluctuated from 12 to 14% in the period 2009–2013 [Statista 2014]. The actual number is probably much higher.

Economy: The economy is dominated by central planning, state ownership of oil and large enterprises, village agriculture, small-scale private retails, and service ventures. Infrastructure has been improving steadily during the past decades, although it is currently affected by inflation and unemployment. The inflation rate was more than 30% in 2012 and now has a slightly downward trend. The service sector contributes to about 47% of the GDP, followed by industry (mining and manufacturing) with 42% and agriculture with 11% [Tandem 2008].

Governance: There are strong national efforts to increase environmental protection and sustainability, to care for ecological necessities, to reduce greenhouse gas emission, and to halt the waste of resources. The subsidies for oil, gas, electricity, and water have been rigorously decreased.

Resources: With nearly 4,000 barrels per day, Iran is the world's fourth largest oil conveyor country. Indeed, the capacity of the refineries in the country lags far behind the crude oil

production, so that predominantly crude oil is exported and refined products have to be reimported.

Initial Situation

The main target of constructing new cities should be the reduction of energy-consumption and greenhouse gas emissions, and the support of good microclimates. On one hand, weather conditions depend on numerous atmospheric factors, such as direct and diffuse radiation, temperature, wind speed and wind direction, relative humidity, and precipitation. On the other hand, there are far too few weather stations in regions like Iran and Egypt. Although the national weather service controls the weather situation with its own stations, due to the insufficient complementary infrastructure, these data are not sufficient for microclimate analysis. In order to analyse the climate, it is important to have dense networks of weather stations that can measure the relevant climate parameters over the entire year. The data obtained are useful to protect human health, to plan new cities, to manage energy supplies, as well as to control climate change. To achieve these aims, it is necessary to increase the

Fig. 2 Dust and air pollution should be avoided in the proximity of a weather station [Author].

number of weather stations to officially measure more data, and to use mobile instruments to measure the temperature, relative humidity, and wind speed in the new city. Urban planners and architects have their own scientific knowledge on how to build a new city, but they need extra information about the weather and especially the microclimate, because these microclimates have a significant impact on people's lives.

Special Background

Climate protection is unpopular in countries like Iran where cheap oil is available. Installing and servicing a meteorological station needs highly qualified experts, as well as skilled workmen. For example, a weather station has to be controlled daily due to dust. Therefore, staff should pass a professional course to give them the necessary skills to work with the highly sensitive instruments. Furthermore, employees should know and understand how data logs function in order to be able to read the data.

Objectives and Targets

The first aim of the project was integrating urban planners to find a suitable site for a weather station. It could encourage an operator to be involved in a project.

Target Groups

Many of the inhabitants of the city were influenced by the activities, and many of them even participated in the project. A weather station is useful for weather forecasting. The measured data can pave the way for analysing microclimates and, along with it, can provide a better quality of life in new towns.

Fig. 3   Finding a suitable site for the weather station [Author]

Fig. 4   Participant taking temperature and humidity data in the city [Author]

Fig. 5   Wind speed measurements at night [Author]

Parties Involved

Researchers from the Freie Universität Berlin, Department of Meteorology developed the station. They briefed the staff and the inhabitants about the weather station and explained the aim of having a mobile measuring campaign in the city.

Subjects, Issues, and Contents

During our case study analysis, we became more familiar with the microclimate of the city, where trees have a great influence. In the current process, inhabitants, especially students, were involved in this project. As a result, the temperature, the relative humidity, and the wind speed were measured in the entire city to find out the criteria of microclimate.

Methods, Scenarios, and Organisation

The measuring campaign should be carried out for at least two weeks. In each 24-hour session during the measuring time, the parameters (temperature, relative humidity, wind speed) were measured six times. The measured data will be used as an input for the micro model ENVI-met to simulate the climate in streets. Several short training sequences were offered, varying from about one to two hours. They were mostly focused on the most important current issues during the measuring time.

Instruments, Products, and Learning

There is one instrument available for measuring the temperature and the relative humidity and one instrument that measures wind speed. Time series of temperature, relative humidity, and wind speed of different regions are available as an input for ENVI-met.

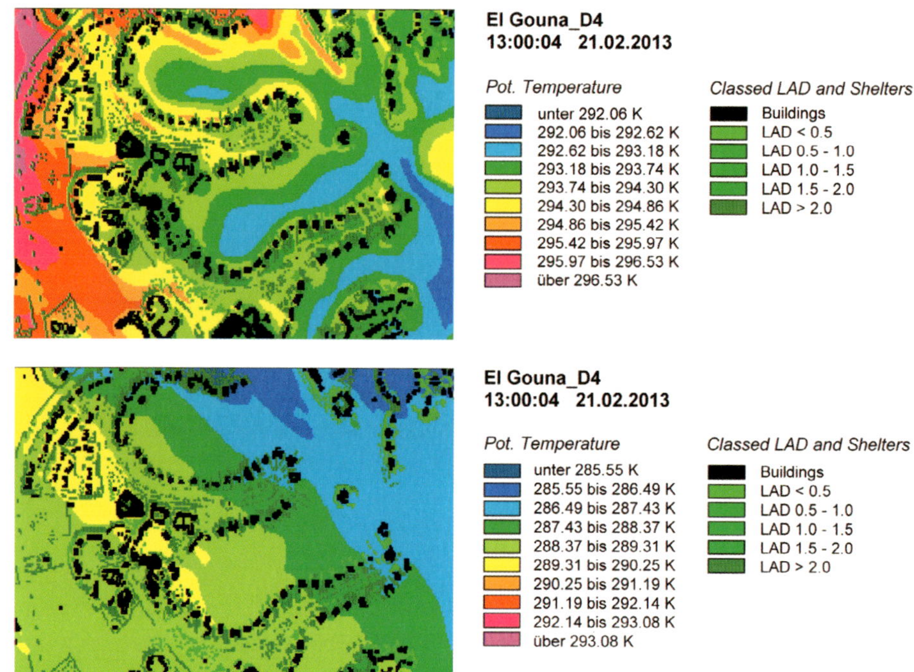

Fig. 7   Microclimate model ENVI-met [Author]

Fig. 8   Setting up the weather station [Author]

Costs, Efforts, Resources, and Preparation

The measuring campaign lasted two weeks. The duration of the training course was one day for trainers and for the coordinators. Their salary and the travel costs also had to be covered. Additionally, there are operation costs for translation and for buying the mobile instruments, as well as for the instruments of the weather station. The overall costs are estimated to be around 45,000 euro, including personal costs.

Essential Requirements

In order to hold the workshops, it is necessary to have a seminar room in close proximity to the area where the measurements will be taken.

Experience

The exemplary meteorological station was built up in EL Gouna, Egypt, because the realisation of the station in Hashtgerd New Town, Iran was unfortunately not possible for administrative, organisational, and financial reasons. The parameters of global and diffuse radiation, wind speed, wind direction, relative humidity, temperature, and the long-wave radiation are measured. Mobile measurements were also taken and a specific part of the city was simulated by the microclimate model ENVI-met.

For more Information

Please contact the author.

References

Gründer, D. (2013): "Validation of ENVI-met for the Lagoon city El Gouna". Bachelor's thesis, Freie Universität Berlin

Huttner, S. (2012): *Further Development and Application of the 3D Microclimate Simulation ENVI-met.* Dissertation, Johannes Gutenberg Universität, Mainz

Notes

1 Cf. Schmidt/Mahrin "On-Site Construction Workshops in Iran" [pp. 85-98 ↗] in this volume.

2 http://www.youngcities.org/151.html

TEHRAN-KARAJ: Construction worker preparing mortar [Mona Navab]

Bernd Mahrin

Complementary Digital and Printed Learning Media on Construction Topics

Keywords

E-Learning
Blended Learning
Digital Learning Media
Instruction Sheets
Learning Videos
Media Mix

Basic Information

Location: Islamic Republic of Iran, Tehran-Karaj Region/Hashtgerd New Town

Climate: The climate in the Tehran-Karaj region is semi-arid.

Geomorphology: The region is heavily endangered by earthquakes.

Ecology: The population's awareness about energy and environment has not yet achieved a desirable level. As result, any efforts have to be supported by education and awareness-raising measures.

Population: Iran's population rose from 67 million inhabitants in 2003 to 80 million today. Of these, 15 million live in the Tehran-Karaj region and 50,000 in Hashtgerd. More than two-thirds of the Iranian people are under the age of thirty.

Education: The literacy rate is 82%. Women compose more than half of the university students. The general education system has improved enormously during the last three decades. Vocational training is strongly focused on academic knowledge and theoretical issues, whilst practical training is commonly disregarded.

Employment: According to official figures, the number of unemployed fluctuated from 12 to 14% in the period 2009–2013 [Statista 2014]. The actual number is probably much higher.

Economy: The economy is dominated by central planning, state ownership of oil and large enterprises, village agriculture, small-scale private retails, and service ventures. Infrastructure has been improving steadily during the past decades, although it is currently affected by inflation and unemployment. The inflation rate was more than 30% in 2012 and now has a slightly downward trend. The service sector contributes to about 47% of the GDP, followed by industry (mining and manufacturing) with 42% and agriculture with 11% [Tandem 2008].

Governance: There are strong national efforts to increase environmental protection and sustainability, to care for ecological necessities, to reduce greenhouse gas emission, and to halt waste of resources. The subsidies for oil, gas, electricity, and water have been rigorously decreased.

Resources: With nearly 4,000 barrels per day, Iran is the world's fourth largest oil conveyor country. Indeed, the capacity of the refineries in the country lags far behind the crude oil production, so that predominantly crude oil is exported and refined products have to be reimported.

Initial Situation

The situation of worker's qualification in Iran's construction industry is hardly comparable to other branches. In general opinion, construction work has a bad reputation and is poorly paid. Therefore, it is often the last choice of occupation [Bagherian/Thorngate 2008]. Many people are convinced that practising construction work does not require any special qualifications or competences. The construction firms have to deal with that situation, but they also caused it. On one hand, the construction industry is interested in skilled workers; on the other hand, the industry's own engagement in human resources management and in vocational training is completely insufficient. Most of the construction firms rarely employ permanent staff at the level of workers. Their interest in better qualified workers is impacted by the fact that workers whose required skills improve try to get higher salaried jobs in other branches, such as the chemical or petroleum industries. Some experts remarked in interviews that even many of the small groups of practically skilled or experienced workers don't put their abilities into practice because it is not valued, since construction firms and building owners fear a loss of profit. Hence, it is not surprising that construction quality and energy efficiency are unacceptable in many residential and office buildings. But the situation at construction sites can be improved by means of qualification with regard to work organisation, logistics, safety, information management, and new technologies and materials, etc.

Special Background

As expected, the field of construction is underrepresented in the Iranian vocational training system [Majedi Ardakani 2009]. The working and learning conditions at the training centres we could visit in the course of the project are acceptable, but the usage of these capacities is insufficient [Schmidt/Mahrin 2013]. Many of the trainers are not familiar with new construction technologies and materials. The type and duration of the training of trainers do not enable them to professionally instruct workers at construction sites. As in many countries, training in Iran is very theoretical. The focus lies on technologies, whilst didactic and pedagogical aspects are widely ignored. There are expandable approaches, but efficient and targeted concepts for systematic apprenticeships and further education in the construction field are missing [cf. Saidi 2003]. Thus, the transferability of the emerged measures and materials in the Young Cities project is most important.

Objectives and Targets

The Young Cities project's sphere of action is too small to inspire a transfer or a reform of the vocational training system. But performing pilot workshops at construction sites, developing training concepts and learning media with a rigorous focus on practical training, examples, methods, and tools can be used for modularised trainings with the aim of a cumulative ho-listic apprenticeship [Rückert et al. 2012]. Thus, learning media production is not only aimed at

Fig. 1   Deficient safety at a Hashtgerd construction site [Navab Motlagh/TU Berlin]

Fig. 2   (left) Instruction of a construction worker at a Hashtgerd construction site [Author]

Fig. 3   (right) Engineering exercise to put glue to an insulation element [Navab Motlagh/TU Berlin]

supporting the project's training workshops, but also at transferring the training concept and contents. The transfer activities (see below) are directed primarily towards Iran, but they are not limited to this country.

Target Groups

The Young Cities training measures were mainly addressed to both certified and uncertified foremen who have to introduce, support, and supervise construction workers. These requirements make immanent shortcomings visible: many of the foremen are neither used to practising construction work themselves, nor do they have the necessary means and resources to train their staff adequately.

Construction workers were the secondary target group [Figure 2 ↗], and they were expected to benefit from the measures at least indirectly. In this group, only a few people have significant practical experience from real construction projects when starting their employment—frequently under very poor life and work conditions. Most are unskilled and are migrant workers from poorer countries in the region. Furthermore, vocational training is made more difficult by cultural differences, language barriers, and lack of literacy skills.

During the Young Cities project, a third potential target group for practical construction training measures arose, namely architects and engineers who had little direct contact with construction work practice during their academic education and during their daily work. Although some of them were very hesitant to participate actively in practice exercises because they are not used to it, they showed keen interest in proper workmanship [Figure 3 ↗].

Parties Involved

The development of the supporting media was inspired by the department of technical didactics of construction technology and landscape design at the Technische Universität Berlin (TU Berlin). The didactic concept and the content were elaborated in close cooperation with the Vocational Advancement Service of the Berlin-Brandenburg Construction Industry Association (BFW BB). Photos and videos were also produced in the framework of this collaboration. The media were developed in consultation with the Road, Housing & Urban Development Research Center of Iran (BHRC, former Building and Housing Research Center). ModernLearning GmbH,[1] based in Berlin, was responsible for the post processing of the media and for the technical production of the online application.

Subjects, Issues, and Contents

The training workshops at Hashtgerd New Town can be seen as the initial point of the training media development. They dealt with several topics,[2] and made practical exercises central. As circumstances required, theoretical background and alternative execution of special work processes were explained and discussed. The language barrier was overcome by a translator. Nevertheless, the lack of adequate learning materials and demonstration objects was a profound barrier to a good learning outcome. To enhance the acquisition and securing of knowledge in the workshops and to support the dissemination of know-how, it seemed appropriate to develop printed and digital media. With a view to the special target group of partly illiterate participants (see above), the media had to be based on pictures and videos, and confined to the proper sequence of work and the essential tools and materials.

Prototypically, online learning media and printed instruction sheets were generated for five subjects:
· Masonry using autoclaved aerated concrete (AAC)
· Installation of windows and doors
· Floating floors/footfall sound insulation
· Indoor plastering
· Applying external thermal insulation composite systems (ETICS)
Within these themes, the media address all essential aspects of the working processes, including very ambitious operations such as aligning window frames [Figure 4a ↗] or placing lintels [Figure 4b ↗], but also very simple tasks such as cleaning used tools [Figure 5a ↗]. In particular, the importance

Fig. 4 (a) Aligning the window frame, (b) Placing a lintel [ModernLearning]

Fig. 5 (a) Cleaning tools, (b) Fixing the reinforcing gauze at the building's corner [ModernLearning]

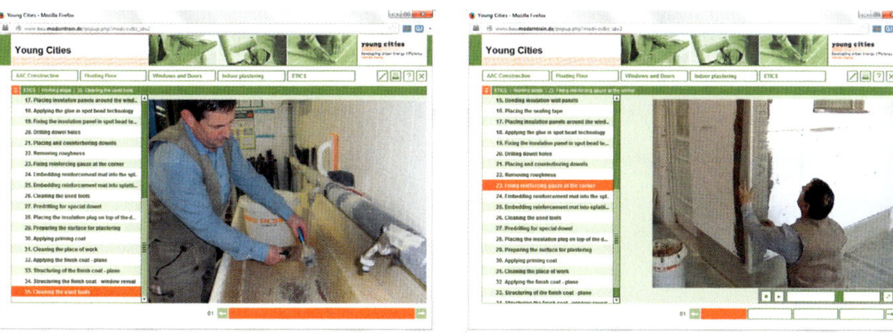

Fig. 6 (a) Selection of tools for AAC masonry, (b) Requested material for a single working step [ModernLearning]

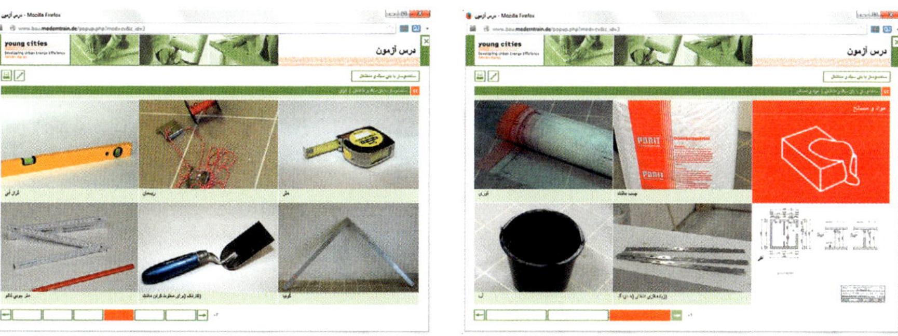

of apparently simple operations and their relationship to the quality of work, sustainability, and cost reduction is often underestimated. With respect to the usual notation system, the screen visualisations in the English version and in the Persian version are right-left reversed.

Instruments, Products, and Learning

First and most importantly, the media that arose from the capacity development dimension within the Young Cities project cannot substitute systematic vocational training and the trainer's and instructor's efforts; but they can support training measures and offer new

Fig. 7 Learning process control [ModernLearning]

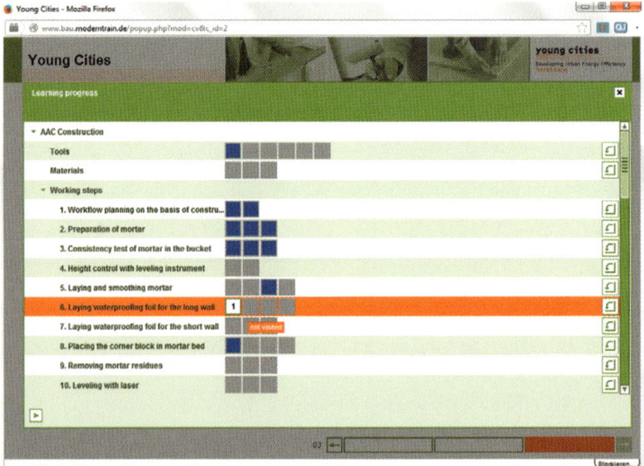

Fig. 8 Fitting windowsill—Sample page from the English version of the instruction sheets [Poor-Rahim]

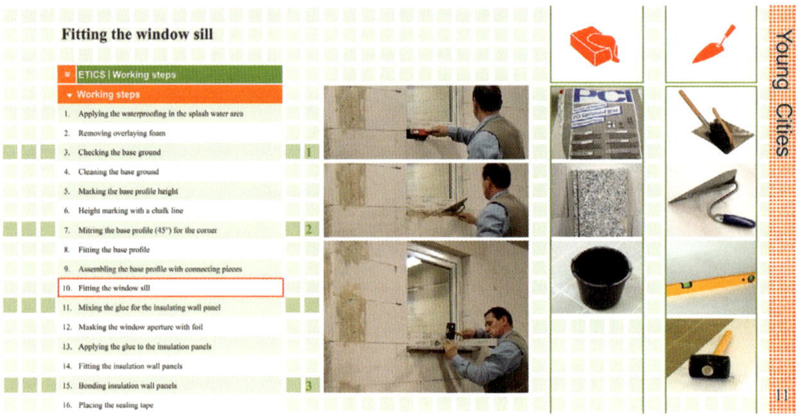

Fig. 9 Floating floor—Sample page from the Persian version of the instruction sheets [Poor-Rahim]

access to complex subjects. As the videos and instruction sheets are in principle available on demand, they uncouple learning processes from fixed places and times given by training organisations or other authorities.

The digital online version has three different content areas at any working step: the video showing the proper execution [Figures 4 and 5 ↗], and two photographic overviews about the necessary tools [Figure 6a ↗] and materials [Figure 6b ↗]. They are complemented by a fourth area giving additional information in written form. The length of the video sequences varies from approximately 15 to 60 seconds. Users quickly receive information about their stage of learning through an easy learning process control [Figure 7 ↗].

In the instruction sheets, the three main content areas are united on one page for each working step [Figures 8 and 9 ↗].

Methods, Scenarios, and Organisation

The two selected media types meet specific and diverse demands concerning the learning and teaching framework:

- The online platform, including more than 130 video sequences, requires the availability of adequate hardware and data connection. In case of a missing online connection, the DVD-based offline version can be used. Regardless of whether the online or the offline is used, the product is suitable in situated learning processes—for example, in seminar rooms, site offices, or similar facilities.[3] The software application is even free for private learning, but only a few of the foreign construction workers in Iran may have access to it.
- The printed material has a very handy format, which makes it usable at construction sites. If any uncertainty comes up about how to do things correctly, the instruction sheet provides clarity with the picture sequences. Yet, it remains a descriptive and representative instrument that does not give any explanation or comment. Nevertheless, it can be very helpful to transfer knowledge, to gain experience, and to avoid serious and costly mistakes.

These easy-to-use products are groundbreaking in this field, because they have been designed and produced to be understood even by people who are functionally illiterate. Both the online learning tools and the printed work step guides are available for each of the subjects mentioned above. In each case, the digital and the printed media are perfectly harmonised in content and design. This is to support successful implementation of newly acquired knowledge into practice of work. By using the instruction sheets as guiding tools to proper workmanship, learning becomes an integrated part of the relevant working processes. But this concept will only work if the instruction sheets are permanently available at the workplace, and if systematic instruction by a trainer or a foreman took place before.

Costs, Efforts, Resources, and Preparation

It was a common interest of all involved parties to devise and to realise the learning media as far as possible out of own resources and by using the existing project budget. The idea behind this decision was to determine if it is possible to produce helpful learning media under ordinary conditions. Concerning concept, didactic design, and production of the micro content like video sequences, photos, and texts, this strategy was realistic and successful given that the Megacities projects already assured a relative convenient framework. However, the creation,

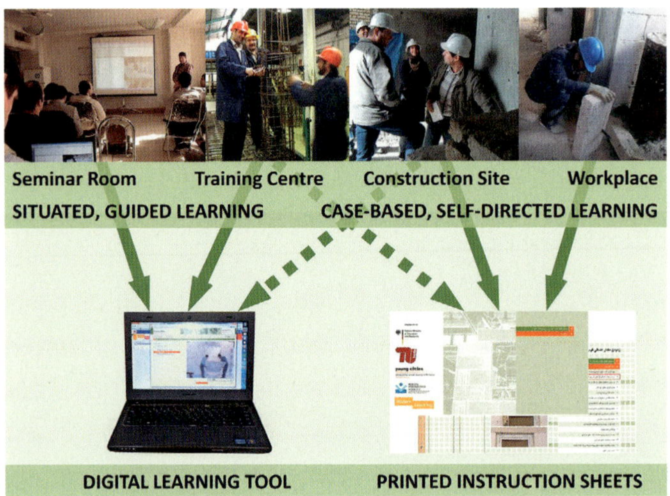

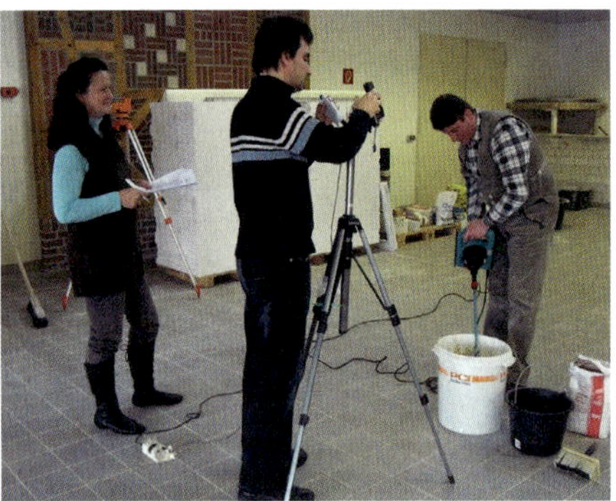

selection, and processing of around 135 short video sequences and hundreds of photographs, and the design of the basic layout was very time-consuming. Overall, it took about three to four person-months. The movies were shot in a training hall of the BFW BB in Frankfurt (Oder) with semi-professional equipment. Including preparation and arrangements, it took one week with five people involved.

The realisation of the online learning platform exceeded both the disposable resources and the technical abilities. Therefore, this job was outsourced to a professional media company. This created—apart from a flawless technical product—two main benefits: the underlying proven and sophisticated author management system ModernWork[4] allows easy system maintenance and adaption to other themes and languages, and makes it possible to create offline versions quite easily.

To sum up, the total costs of the described digital and printed media is estimated at 50,000 euro—including imputed costs of the own contributions. This is a comparatively low expense considering that a lot of worthwhile material came into existence and can be spread across Iran and other countries.

Essential Requirements

The necessary technical and personnel resources to develop learning media as described depend not only on the type, complexity, extent, and required technical quality of the aspired products; much also depends on the didactical background and the media competencies of the involved people. Setting up a project like this needs broad experience in media design, creating storyboards, producing and post-processing audio-visual content. In case of the limited experience in media development and use in learning environments and sceneries, assistance and support by media professionals and didactic experts is strongly recommended.

There is a good alternative to videos with regard to keeping the efforts and expenses within limits, especially when starting media use in vocational training: instead of shooting movie sequences, it is possible to create "digital stories" and restrict them to the media formats–including photos, graphics, text, and podcasts–depending of the literacy of the target groups.[5]

Experiences

The testing of the final versions of the digital learning media and the printed instruction sheets within the Young Cities project could only take place on a small scale. This is due to the fact that the media development was an additional activity, which came up during the running project. Thus, the media products were finished not long before the project's end. They were committed to the Iranian partners for approval and transfer.

Contemporaneously, test runs with participants from Eastern Europe states took place at the BFW-BB vocational training centres in Cottbus and Frankfurt (Oder). The results were, without exception, very positive.

Implementation

Transfer and implementation are to be carried out by the Road, Housing & Urban Development Research Center of Iran. Furthermore, the Iranian Technical and Vocational Training Organization will be involved in the implementation process.

Transfer and Dissemination Activities

The media are intended for publication and are already available free of charge in English and Persian:
- The web-based learning platform is available at http://www.bau.moderntrain.de/. Login is requested either with the guest account (guest/guest) or with an individual account that will be created on demand. It is planned to move this comprehensive didactic product to the project's website www.youngcities.org, and in cooperation with the transnational partners to an Iranian server. This may help to offer the learning tool to a wider circle of users.
- An offline version of the platform is available on DVD and can be obtained on demand at the German and Iranian project partner institutions.
- The five instruction sheets and a guideline for checking construction sites are available for free download as printable PDF files at http://www.youngcities.org/137.html. They will also be printed as brochures.

Currently, in the framework of one of the Megacities' flagship projects, plans are to adapt the instruction sheets concept to the subject of installing automatic mechanical ventilation systems.[6] This new product will be disseminated by Chinese construction firms.

In the project "WEB-TT Water Energy Building–Training and Transfer",[7] one of the BMBF-funded VET export projects, and running in cooperation with the Egyptian construction industry, the transfer of the concept, and the adaption of the learning media are under discussion.

Moreover, the specially modified media concept was presented and discussed with experts at several meetings, conferences, and similar occasions. The networking conferences and thematic symposia organised by the Fraunhofer-Zentrum für Mittel- und Osteuropa (MOEZ)[8] are to be mentioned particularly.

References

Bagherian, F./Thorngate, W. (2008). "Iran". In: McCulloch, G.; Crook, D. (Eds.): *The Routledge International Encyclopedia of Education.* Abingdon, Oxon, pp. 324–25

Mahrin, B./Schmidt, K./Poor-Rahim, N. (2013): *Instruction Sheets: AAC Construction, Floating Floor, Windows and Doors, Indoor Plastering,* ETICS. Berlin, Technische Universität Berlin und Berufsförderungswerk e.V. des Bauindustrieverbands Berlin-Brandenburg e.V. (Eds.). www.youngcities.org/137.html (27.02.2014)

Majedi Ardakani, M.H. (2009): *Probleme der technischen und beruflichen Ausbildung.* Contribution to Young Cities project meeting, Building and Housing Research Center (BHRC), Tehran

Rückert, K./Grunwald, J./Mahrin, B. (2011): „Pilot Project New Quality". In: Schäfer, R./Nasrollahi, F./Ohlenburg, H./Stellmacher, F. (Eds.): *Accomplishments and Objectives. Young Cities Research Paper Series,* Volume 02. Berlin, Teheran. Universitätsverlag Technische Universität Berlin, pp. 90–94

Saidi, K. (2003). *Iranian National Masterplan for a Labour Market Oriented Job Training System.* Discussion paper, Tehran, gtz

Schmidt, K./Mahrin, B. (2013): "Results from Construction Site Visits and Expert Talks". In: Mahrin, B./Meyser, J. (Eds.): *Construction Competencies and Building Quality–Case Study Results.* Young Cities Research Paper Series, Volume 06. Universitätsverlag Technische Universität Berlin, pp. 18–27

Notes

1 http://modernlearning.de/en.html

2 They are described in Schmidt/Mahrin "On-Site Construction Workshops in Iran" [pp. 85-98 ↗] in this volume.

3 See for instance Poor-Rahim/Mahrin "Mobile Learning Containers (MLC) for Improving the Qualification of Workers at Construction Sites" [pp. 46-58 ↗] in this volume.

4 http://modernlearning.de/en

5 For further interesting hints on digital storytelling, please see https://en.wikipedia.org/wiki/Digital_storytelling (last view 27.03.2014).

6 Cf. Franke et al. "Training on the Way to the First Passive House in Western China" [pp. 131-140 ↗] in this volume.

7 www.web-tt.org/

8 http://berufsbildungsexport-meta.de/

PROJECTS IN BRIEF

On the following pages, all nine participating cities of the research programme on Future Megacities are presented. They were funded between 2008–2013. Details are collected about the context and challenges for the projects, their objectives, and approaches. A short overview of the most important outcomes and solutions is provided. More information on these solutions can be found in the Products and Tools Data Base at www.future-megacities.org.

Featured in this volume:
Adaptation Planning in Ho Chi Minh City (Vietnam)
Energy and Climate Protection in Gauteng (South Africa)
New Town Development in Tehran-Karaj Region (Iran)
Water Management in Lima (Peru)
Urban Agriculture in Casablanca (Morocco)
Solid Waste Management in Addis Ababa (Ethiopia)
Resource Efficiency in Urumqi (China)
Governance for Sustainability in Hyderabad (India)

Featured in other volumes:
Transportation Management in Hefei (China)

Energy and Climate Protection in Gauteng (South Africa)

Context

Gauteng Province in South Africa is the most densely urbanised area in South Africa and covers an area of 18,178 km^2. The province consists of the three large metropolises: Johannesburg, Ekurhuleni, and Tshwane, as well as two other district municipalities. Most of the province is located at an average altitude of 1,500 m above sea level, with high solar radiation levels. There has been a striking lack of energy-supply security over the last years, with frequent blackouts hindering Gauteng's aim to be competitive as a global city. The energy-supply system is dominated by electricity generated from coal. About one-third of the fuel for transport is also produced from coal. Gauteng's levels of energy consumption and gas emissions can be compared to that of developed countries like Germany. For the energy sector alone, the energy consumption in 2009 was 765 PJ and the total CO_2 emissions were 126 million tonnes (10.5 tonnes per person). Despite the high solar radiation, the share of renewable-energy use remains low. Due to low costs for electricity (relative to international costs), there are few incentives for energy-saving behaviour and a more energy-efficient policy implementation.

Objectives

The EnerKey project intends to contribute to a sustainable transformation of the Gauteng urban area by developing an integrated programme for an efficient, environmentally friendly, and climate-protecting system of energy supply and utilisation. EnerKey supports this process by carrying out research and assisting stakeholders in the implementation and monitoring of projects, measures, and strategies. This includes the development and application of tools and instruments for energy and environmental planning. Providing training and education courses to staff and administration members of the municipalities will enable capacity building and dissemination of the results. The specific objectives are:

1. Assess the present values of energy consumption and GHG emissions of the energy system in Gauteng
2. Provide means to improve the energy performance in the building sector, especially in public buildings
3. Initiate a process to reduce energy consumption and related emissions from traffic and transport
4. Show viable options for using more renewable energy
5. Demonstrate, with a number of practical projects, that the implementation of sustainable projects makes sense and can be successful

Approach

The EnerKey project has a clear interdisciplinary and integrated approach by combining socio-economic and technical aspects, as well as by cooperating with partners from different departments of regional and municipal authorities, NGOs, the private sector, and universities. The project follows both a "top-down" and a "bottom-up" approach. In the short term, individual pilot projects are being initiated, for example, in schools, administrative buildings, and in the transport sector. These projects are developed and monitored with the help of decision support tools and models. In parallel, an integrated energy model approach is set up, resulting in the provision of measures and recommendations to improve urban development and the energy system in the region. The EnerKey project specifically undertakes measures for strengthening the Gauteng regional administration, to coordinate the municipal efforts in energy planning and in the development of pilot projects. Training and capacity building are undertaken to disseminate the results and findings.

School project on potentials of energy saving in Gauteng [Carsten Zehner]

Solutions

- Gauteng Energy Office—the regional answer to energy challenges
- TIMES GECCO—A regional energy- and emission-cost optimisation model and training
- EnerKey Advisor Tool—assessing energy performance of buildings
- EnerKey Long Term Perspective Group—a government think-tank model
- Transport Emission Inventory—informed mobility planning
- Energy Technology Handbook—sustainable technologies for the future
- CDM—Emission Trade Evaluation Tool
- iEEECo—energy awareness activities for scholars and cost-efficient settlements for the poor
- African Sustainable House—a holistic dwelling approach
- EnerKey "Detectives"—education and installation of solar panels in schools
- EnerKey Environmental and Energy Atlas— Assessment of Renewable Energy options for the Gauteng Province

Contact

Project: EnerKey-Energy as a key element of an integrated climate protection concept for the city region of Gauteng
Ludger Eltrop | IER—University of Stuttgart
Email: ludger.eltrop@ier.uni-stuttgart.de
Harold Annegarn | University of Johannesburg
Email: hannegarn@gmail.com
Webpage: www.enerkey.info, www.enerkey.co.za, www.enerkey.de

Solid Waste Management in Addis Ababa (Ethiopia)

Context

Addis Ababa is one of the fastest-growing cities in Africa and also the main commercial, financial, industrial, and service-provision centre in Ethiopia. The city is presently facing a plethora of problems, including insufficient solid, and liquid-waste management. While an ever-increasing volume of waste is generated, the effectiveness of the solid waste collection and disposal systems is declining.

In Addis Ababa, around 80% of the solid waste produced is collected. The remaining waste is dumped on open spaces or drains. The city has separate systems available that handle solid wastes. The formal system managed by the city administration collects the waste from collection points and transfers it to the landfill site (secondary collection). The second system assembles groups of organised precollectors who collect the waste from households and bring it to the collection points (primary collection). The collection of recyclables is performed by so-called korales, who collect only a small percentage of recyclables directly from the households. Both the precollectors and the korales are physically, socially, and economically disadvantaged waste workers, whose work compensates for the lack of municipal services. Up to now, the recycling sector in Addis Ababa, particularly for organic waste, remains undeveloped.

This means that organic waste, which makes up more than 60% of the municipal solid waste, is simply collected and dumped in the landfill. The landfill gas generated by the organic waste is not collected either, thus contributing significantly to the greenhouse gas emissions of the city.

Objectives

The general objective of the IGNIS project is to demonstrate that waste, if it is understood and treated as a resource, can be a source for income generation and can contribute to global climate-protection, as well as to local environmental protection and sustainable development. Hence, the project aims to generate income from valorising municipal solid waste through establishing qualified, economically workable, and sustainable waste treatment. Furthermore, the project seeks to contribute directly to poverty reduction and improved sanitation, and, moreover, to reducing greenhouse gases from dumpsites, conserving raw materials, and improving energy and resource efficiency.

In this context, the project aims to provide an instrument that includes methods, practical approaches, and simulation tools to be applied to other emerging megacities, in order to assess the effects when introducing similar waste management and treatment methods.

Approach

The approach comprises different strategies that correlate with one another. An essential aspect of the project's approach is the generation of a reliable spatial, waste, and emission database for the scientific work and the calculations of various scenarios. Additionally, pilot projects have been implemented and will be developed further. The majority of these pilot projects are small-scale projects on a decentralised level (e.g., composting, anaerobic digestion, recycling). These pilot projects are analysed with a focus on technical, greenhouse gas, and emission-related, socio-economic, and occupational safety and health (OSH) related aspects. Furthermore, the scientific staff, the city administration, and the groups working on the pilot projects are given the opportunity to build capacities and become familiar with the technologies as well as with the concept of using waste as a resource.

The data collected and the results of the pilot project analyses are used for modelling, simulation, or up-scaling of the businesses. Scenario simulation will provide the possibility of showing the

The paper manufacture of Tesfaye Mekonnen partly uses waste as raw material [Lukas Born].

effects, for example, on greenhouse gases and the socio-economy. IGNIS is not conceived as a specific, isolated solution for Addis Ababa. Rather, several aspects of the project—e.g., methods—pilot projects, results, and lessons learnt, are transferred to other fast-growing cities in order to learn from the specific requirements of those cities. As a result, the IGNIS approach will be modified and adapted accordingly.

Solutions

- Methodology for data collection on waste quantities and quality
- Model-based strategic planning for sustainable solid waste management
- Adapted occupational safety and health standards and solutions
- Market studies and business guidelines for entrepreneurs and for recycling products
- Business improvement options for a paper-recycling manufacturer
- Implementation projects for separate collection at source, biogas facility, charcoal briquettes from organic wastes, composting, school biogas-latrine
- Training modules for WEEE collection and dismantling
- Closing material cycles by means of using biogas sludge for erosion-prevention combined with energy crop production
- Obstacle-based transfer analysis methodology for technologies or methods

Contact

Project: IGNIS—Income generation & climate protection by valorising municipal solid wastes in a sustainable way in emerging mega-cities
Dieter Steinbach | AT-Verband Stuttgart
Email: dieter.steinbach@at-verband.de
Webpage: www.ignis.p-42.net

Urban Agriculture in Casablanca (Morocco)

Context

Casablanca, currently the largest and most populated urban region in Morocco, has grown within a mere century from a small settlement of 20,000 inhabitants to a metropolis of estimated 5.1 million by 2030. 22% of the national urban population live in Casablanca. 60% of industry in Morocco is concentrated in this agglomeration—creating rapid urban growth, accompanied by the development of deprived quarters (*bidonvilles*). In 1907, the city covered a small area of only fifty hectares. In 1997, the region "Greater Casablanca" was created comprising 121,412 ha and 8 prefectures. Thus, many previously rural communities with agricultural areas are being urbanised, thereby consuming valuable open space. As a resulting phenomenon of current development processes specific to megacities, Urban Agriculture (UA) as a spatial dimension is considered to present new hybrid and climate-sensitive forms between rural and urban space. An underlying hypothesis is that these reciprocal urban-rural linkages contain the potential for a qualified coexistence that could be the basis for forming sustainable climate-optimised, multifunctional urban and open spatial structures (productive landscapes) in order to make a long-term contribution to the sustainability of cities and the quality of life for their inhabitants. It is to be assumed that UA will only be able to coexist in the long term and in a qualitatively meaningful manner with other, economically stronger forms of land utilisation, when synergies between urban and agricultural uses arise.

Objectives

The project explores the existence of synergies between urban and agricultural uses and investigates how they might be developed. The project focuses on the possibilities of integrating peri-urban agricultural land into the urban development process.

It also analyses the extent to which UA can make a relevant contribution to a climate-optimised and sustainable urban development as an integrative factor in urban growth centres. It aims to answer the following research questions:

1. To what extent can UA play a significant role in adapting to the consequences of climate change, via climate protection, and via energy efficiency?
2. To what extent is UA an innovative strategy for sustainable land conservation of open urban areas?
3. To what extent can UA contribute to the struggle against poverty?
4. How can UA be integrated into urban development as a vital element in accordance with local conditions?

Approach

The parallel development of a theoretical basis, basic research, and applied research and implementation strategies characterises the project. The research team is bi-national, interdisciplinary, and transdisciplinary. The project pursues an open, process-oriented research approach subjected to follow-up adjustments.

According to the methodological approaches of the participating research disciplines, subsidiary research approaches follow different routes, comprising the normative, the descriptive/empirical, and the applied research orientation. The three most important methodological tools for the overall project are the spiral-shaped work approach, the integration of the subsidiary results, and the action-research approach via the pilot projects. The four topics urban development, agriculture, climate change and governance, and technical support were defined for the organisation of the working process and were studied in depth.

Environmental education starts with a passionate teacher in a school of Casablanca [Lukas Born].

Solutions

- Action Plan for integrating UA into the urban development process
- Design solutions for multifunctional space systems
- Models of regional and local climate, weather, water balance, air quality, and flooding as a basis for informed decision-making
- Experimental plants for industrial wastewater treatment and reuse
- Concepts for peri-urban tourism
- Approaches for healthy food production
- UA as an integrated element in informal settlements
- Awareness-raising (e.g., public campaign) and dissemination strategy

Contact

Project: Urban agriculture as integrative factor of climate-optimised urban development
Undine Giseke | Technische Universität Berlin, Chair of Landscape Architecture/Open Space Planning (TU Berlin)
Email: undine.giseke@tu-berlin.de
Webpage: www.uac-m.org

New Town Development in the Tehran-Karaj Region (Iran)

Context

The enormous increases in population in threshold and developing countries in relation to rapid urbanisation, as well as rising living standards, pose significant challenges to the affected regions in terms of energy supply and climate protection. However, these rapidly growing regions also offer a great potential for shaping sustainable urban development. Particularly in Iran, these developments are strikingly manifest. The Tehran-Karaj region forms one of the fastest-growing urban agglomerations in the Middle East and is a major regional contributor to climate change. There is a demand for the construction of 1.5 million new housing units per year in a country that will be particularly affected by the effects of climate change. With the construction of new settlements, consumption of energy, commodities, and resources is rising dramatically. The related harmful climatic effects intensify global and regional risks.

Objectives

The Young Cities project is a German-Iranian applied research project that aims to develop solutions and strategies for a sustainable, energy-efficient, and resilient urban development in arid and semi-arid regions as a contribution to significant CO_2 reduction. The focus lies on contemporary, formally planned, mass housing, within the framework of the case study of Hashtgerd New Town in Tehran province. The project intends to decrease CO_2 emissions by reducing energy consumption within the principles of sustainable urban development. The aim is to help to reduce the consumption of other valuable environmental resources, primarily water, but also soil and air. These aspects are complemented by taking into account economic and social ambitions including social issues, efficient and flexible management, public participation, and environmentally conscious consumer behaviour, as well as by encouraging a positive local identity.

Approach

To implement the goals and objectives of the project, an integral, interdisciplinary approach to urban development was chosen, ranging across different levels and scales:

- Space—urban structure down to the sub-neighbourhood level
- Networks—infrastructure networks of energy, water, mobility
- Objects—buildings with a variety of different uses

The social and economic conditions of the project are addressed by the further dimension of cross-sector approaches. This part of the approach focuses on high-potential fields of action for sustainable development such as the following:

- Raising the qualification levels of construction workers for better construction quality, thus lowering energy demand of the buildings,
- The participation of the inhabitants and the raising of awareness on environmentally friendly behaviour.

The Young Cities project is committed to Action Research based on the method of "research through design": the verification of research hypotheses through planning, implementation, and realisation of pilot projects forms an integral part of the project. One area, 35 ha in size, located in Hashtgerd New Town, 70 km west of Tehran, has been chosen as the central demonstration site for the development of an energy-efficient neighbourhood, called the "Shahre Javan Community".

Solutions

- Detailed master plan for a 35-ha pilot area; the Shahre Javan Community in Hashtgerd New Town
- "New Quality Building" with sixteen housing units, inaugurated in July 2010
- Manual for a climate-responsive and sustainable urban development

Typical Iranian steel frame construction at Hashtgerd New Town to avoid earthquake damages [Lukas Born]

- Manual for integrated urban planning in semi-arid and arid regions
- Conceptual designs for energy-efficient residential and commercial buildings
- On-site vocational education and training for construction workers
- Public transport concept
- Wastewater concept
- Ecological assessment model
- Implementation of environmental compensation areas

Contact

Project: Young Cities—Developing energy-efficient urban fabric in the Tehran-Karaj region
Rudolf Schäfer | Technische Universität Berlin
School of Planning, Building, Environment
Email: rudolf.schaefer@tu-berlin.de
Webpage: www.youngcities.de

Resource Efficiency in Urumqi (China)

Context

Urumqi is the capital of China's North West Province, "Xinjiang Uygur Autonomous Region" (XUAR). With an initial population of 88,000 inhabitants in 1949, Urumqi is fast becoming the biggest economic growth node in Central Asia, with around 3.1 million inhabitants in the city and about 4.5 million in greater Urumqi. This rapid development is taking place in an ecologically highly sensitive (semi-)arid environment within a 50-km-wide irrigated green belt between the foothills of the glacial Tianshan Ridge (up to 5,445 m a.s.l.) and the Junggar Basin (500–600 m a.s.l.) The cold winters are typically accompanied by extended periods of stable inversion layers, which lead to dramatic increased levels of air pollution. As the region is extremely mineral-rich (coal, oil, gas, ores), dynamic industrialisation and the rising wealth of the growing population, as well as the increasing volume of traffic, are further driving factors that have catapulted Urumqi onto the "blacklist" of the top five most air-polluted cities in the world [Blacksmith Report, 2007]. Both industrial and private household waste are increasing rapidly, not only in quantity but also in variety, without having led to specific adaptations in waste management.

Water is the most precious and socially sensitive resource in the region. A water provision gap starts to open up during the summer months and has to be gradually closed by the (over)exploitation of ground-water resources. Climate change is aggravating the situation, as the snowline rises, the period of snow coverage decreases, as does the period of permanent melted-ice water-runoff in spring.

Objectives

The project concentrates on energy efficiency, water resource efficiency and materials efficiency. Within the overall objective to promote a sustainability-oriented megacity development in semi-arid areas, the project aims to do the following:

- Lower energy consumption in private households, as well as in industrial areas, thereby lowering air pollution, CO_2 emissions, and resource extraction
- Promote the installation of renewable energy-based facilities
- Implement a GPR-based monitoring system, concentrating on soil moisture content as an indicator for climate change
- Design a realistic descriptive hydrological model and decision-making support system for Urumqi to allow political actors to be able to better predict future scenarios and their consequences on water availability and distribution
- Promote developments towards a circular economy on the level of industrial enterprises as well as industrial parks

Approach

The main focal points of the project are directed at the ecologically sensitive and closely interrelated core cycles (1) water, (2) materials, and (3) energy with three Sino-German task groups being assigned respectively. The Chinese teams are led by key political or scientific decision-makers who promote specific tasks based on high-ranking political contacts and who negotiate agreements, which has proven to be a helpful support for the project. Scientists, engineers, and other employees on the execution level proved to be important key partners within the development phase of products, processes, and the specification of advanced new ideas that contribute to greater resource efficiency in the respective fields of action. A cross-cutting exchange of ideas, concepts, and theoretical and practical solutions is being facilitated by various exchange activities.

Groundbreaking ceremony for Urumqi's first passive house [Bernd Mahrin]

Solutions

- Construction of the first passive house in Western China
- Extra low-energy renovation of existing buildings
- Development of waste management software for enterprises in Midong Industrial Park that covers, classifies, and characterises all categories of waste
- Hydrological analyses and modelling, advice on efficient water use, and water information management for political decision-makers in Urumqi Region
- Mass and energy flow analysis in the Chinese PVC industry
- Capacity building for a soil moisture-based measurement methodology (Ground Penetrating Radar) as a basis for modelling climate change

Contact

Project: RECAST Urumqi—Meeting the resource efficiency challenge in a climate-sensitive, dryland megacity

Thomas Sterr | Ruprecht-Karls-Universität Heidelberg, Dept. of Geography

Email: thomas.sterr@geog.uni-heidelberg.de

Webpage: www.urumqi-drylandmegacity.uni-hd.de

Transportation Management in Hefei (China)

Context

Growing urbanisation and the increasing size of metropolitan regions are a challenge, as well as an opportunity, for the economic development and the social balance of societies, particularly in rapidly developing countries like China. The dynamic evolution of Chinese cities poses special challenges for transport concepts. According to the recent census, five million people live in Hefei (capital of Anhui province, China), three million of whom live in the urban area. Meanwhile, the rapid rise of car ownership in Chinese cities significantly impacts people's lifestyles as well as the environment. Traffic congestion as a phenomenon has extended from first-tier cities to second-tier cities such as Hefei. The rapid growth of private car ownership has also led to the excessive rise in road construction which remains insufficient to keep up with traffic growth, while simultaneously consuming valuable land resources in Hefei. Traffic congestion is becoming increasingly critical day by day and causes more delays, fuel consumption, air pollution, and CO_2 emissions. The rapidly growing demand for mobility and housing has created new challenges for urban administrative institutions, which have to deal with an unprecedented urban growth, thus leading to an urgent need for sustainable development.

Objectives

The main objectives of the METRASYS project are to contribute to climate protection through the development of sustainable transport in highly dynamic economic and urban regions. In particular, the project aims to provide decision-makers with the necessary means to effectively implement and guide sustainable transport in Hefei. Furthermore, special emphasis is placed on the general transferability of development approaches on traffic management for comparable megacities worldwide.

Approach

The project integrates different disciplines—e.g., spatial planning, transport science, engineering science, and political science—and addresses both planning and operational aspects of the transport sector, through deployment of a sophisticated geographic information system (GIS) and an advanced traffic-management system. This system also facilitates environmental evaluations and analyses with an emission and pollution dispersion model developed in this project. This, in turn, provides valuable feedback to the transport and urban planning process. Furthermore, the results are used to explore opportunities for climate finance, which provides additional incentives for sustainable transport development. This comprehensive approach was devised and has been implemented in close cooperation with relevant Chinese stakeholders. This contributes to a constructive and concrete stakeholder dialogue, bringing all relevant parties together, thereby addressing the challenges of sustainable mobility in a holistic manner. The project works in four main research areas related to energy-efficient future megacities:

1. Technology Development: Realisation of effective concepts and implementation of intelligent traffic management based on Floating Car Data (FCD) and video detection for intersection monitoring.
2. Model Development: Energy efficiency and reduction of greenhouse gas emissions by assessing the environmental impact of the traffic-management system and the planned urban traffic development through the validation and optimisation process using various models, such as traffic models, emission, and immission models.
3. Transport Planning: Capacity building and accompanying urban and transport planning for sustainable city development.

Inside Hefei's Intelligent Traffic Control Center [Carsten Zehner]

4. Climate Finance: Identification of climate finance opportunities for sustainable low-carbon transport in Hefei.

Solutions

- Intelligent traffic management system based on floating-car data, video detection, and broadcasting with Digital Audio Broadcast (DAB)
- Model development for the assessment of environmental impacts of traffic as a basis for informed decision-making and climate-friendly transport planning strategies
- Guidelines and manuals for best practice in "traffic management", "transport planning", and "urban block design"
- Finance options for sustainable transport
- Strategic design proposal for pedestrian-friendly cities

Contact

Project: METRASYS—Sustainable mobility for megacities
Alexander Sohr | German Aerospace Centre, Institute of Transportation Systems
Email: alexander.sohr@dlr.de
Webpage: www.metrasys.de

Governance for Sustainability in Hyderabad (India)

Context

Greater Hyderabad is predicted to reach a population of 10.5 million inhabitants by 2015. The rapid economic growth of the emerging megacity has facilitated higher living standards and modern lifestyles for the emerging middle class. This is, however, accompanied by escalating energy and resource consumption. Furthermore, long-standing problems remain unresolved. For example, approximately one-third of the population lives below the poverty line and continues to suffer from food, housing, education, and health problems. In addition to this, climate change is predicted to lead to extreme weather events, disastrous floods, strong heat waves, extreme droughts, and increasing water scarcity.

Given this natural, social, and economic context of Hyderabad, the question arises: what can be considered a reasonable response to the anticipated impact of climate change?

Objectives

The overall objective of the project is to develop a sustainable development framework for Hyderabad by prioritising mitigation and adaptation strategies for climate change and energy efficiency.

Focusing on the sectors of transport, food, land-use planning, and the provision of energy and water, the project pursues the following functional objectives:

1. To increase scientific knowledge and to generate a database concerning climate change, its mitigation and adaptation opportunities, as well as to ascertain the potential of energy efficiency through collaborative research.

2. To identify institutional and policy solutions to encourage the change of behaviour of relevant actors in order to address the problems (i.e. "getting the institutions right").

3. To design, propose, and implement demonstrable strategies for climate-change adaptation and mitigation, as well as for increased energy efficiency.

4. To ensure a wider adoption of these strategies by all relevant stakeholders and actors through appropriate communication, capacity building, advocacy, policy dialogues, and dissemination mechanisms.

Approach

The project aims to achieve climate-change adaptation and mitigation, as well as energy efficiency, through the design of appropriate policies that aim to change behaviour. Analysis of policies, of lifestyles in private households, of authorities for urban planning and administration, and of governance structures were conducted in tandem with a technical analysis in each of the focus fields: energy and water supply, food and health, and transport. The results of both analyses guided the conceptualisation of the pilot projects. The project applies a "discourse approach" to implement the necessary changes in the institutions and government organisations. The knowledge generated through the research and the implemented pilot projects that involve all the stakeholders and actors is embedded in local discourse and dialogue.

Eight pilot projects have been implemented and evaluated in the areas of urban planning, transport, food, and clean and efficient energy provision, as well as education for sustainable lifestyles. The management options that evolved through pilot projects have been transferred to relevant stakeholders in Hyderabad with the help of capacity building measures. The consortium, involving partners from scientific, governmental, non-governmental, and private organisations, has formulated a Perspective Action Plan (PAP) for Hyderabad and proposed its adoption.

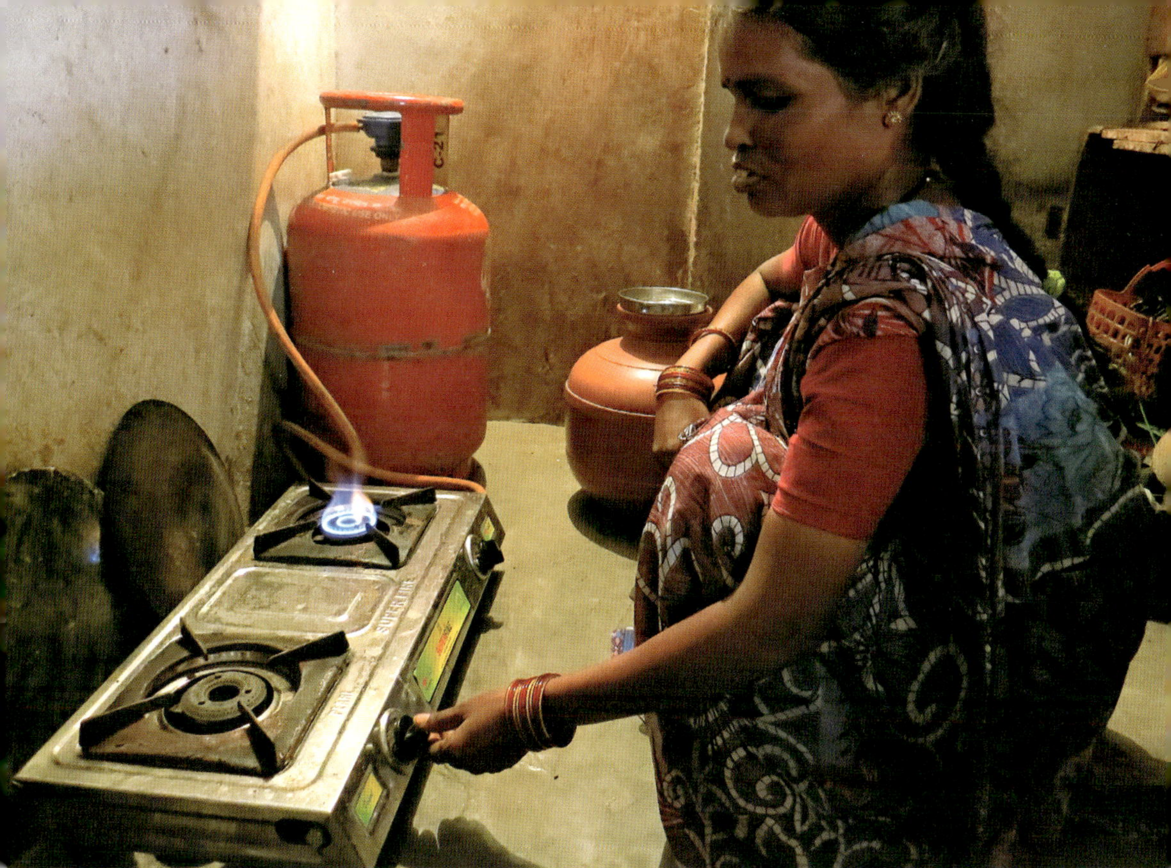

Participant of the collective action for fuel transition among urban poor [Carsten Zehner]

Solutions

- Climate Assessment Tool for Hyderabad (CATHY)
- Strategic Transport Planning Tool
- Street food-safety manual and on-site training to strengthen a climate-friendly urban food-supply system
- Collective action for fuel transition among the urban poor
- Cooperative and technical solutions to increase energy efficiency in irrigation
- Solar powered schools
- Education for sustainable lifestyles
- Community radio

Contact

Project: Climate and energy in a complex transition process towards sustainable Hyderabad—mitigation and adaptation strategies by changing institutions, governance structures, lifestyles, and consumption patterns

Konrad Hagedorn | Humboldt University Berlin, Department of Agricultural Economics
Email: k.hagedorn@agrar.hu-berlin.de
Webpage: www.sustainable-hyderabad.de

Adaptation Planning in Ho Chi Minh City (Vietnam)

Context

The mega-urban region of Ho Chi Minh City (HCMC) in South Vietnam is one of the most dynamic examples of rapid urban development over the last two decades and, therefore, one of the regions most affected by climate change and risks in Vietnam. The urbanisation of Ho Chi Minh City has been intrinsically related to the process of industrialisation following the Doi Moi reforms of market liberalisation in 1987. Between 1986 and 2010, the population of HCMC almost doubled from 3.78 million inhabitants to the current level of 7.4 million inhabitants. In response to this high urbanisation pressure, HCMC's government was forced to repeatedly expand the urban boundary, leading to the establishment of six new urban districts. Due to HCMC's geographical location in a low altitude, intra-tropical coastal zone, northeast of the Mekong Delta and 50 km inland from the South China Sea, the city experiences significant annual variations of climatic and weather extremes. Together with its huge population, its economic assets, and the dominant role it plays in the national economy, the city is considered to be highly vulnerable to the impacts of climate change.

Objectives

The project aims to increase the resilience and adaptation capacities of HCMC in order to reduce the vulnerability of natural and human systems to the adverse effects of climate change. Hence, risks and vulnerabilities are assessed and sustainable adaptation measures are developed and incorporated into urban decision-making and planning processes. Consequently, the project seeks to establish a multi-layered, typological approach, which will be utilised to assess the sustainability of urban settlement developments. Furthermore, the project aims to develop adaptation strategies and measures which can be transferred to other affected regions.

Approach

The project follows an interdisciplinary approach by combining expertise in different fields related to the two overall topics which constitute the project structure: Action Field One focuses on environmental research; Action Field Two focuses on urban development.

The Urban Typology Framework provides important environmental and social information, which, in turn, is referred to the vulnerability assessment, based on strategic environmental assessment (SEA) as a basis for transferring scientifically known and documented problems of climate change into adapted planning systems (Action Field 1). Furthermore, the project aims to bring sustainable urban development strategies, in the context of climate change, into the mainstream urban system of HCMC. Based on the knowledge gained from the research, small-scale projects will be conducted with the Vietnamese partners to promote best-practice methods for further appropriate action (Action Field 2).

On the practical level, the instruments of zoning and building codes will be examined and recommendations will be made for their improvement with regard to sustainable urban development, energy efficiency, and resiliency to adverse climate changes. Furthermore, as the project follows an applied research approach, results are requested in terms of both implementation (practice) and research (theory). Both are complementary; thus, on the one hand, the implementation of measures will be an outcome of scientific research, and, on the other hand, research will be undertaken on the basis of the implementation of measures.

The *Handbook on Green Housing* shows engery-efficient building solutions for private house owners [Carsten Zehner].

Solutions

The following products are results of pilot projects implemented with different target groups:

- Urban Climate Map as a basis for planning decisions within the general land-use plan
- Urban Water Balance Modelling and Planning recommendations
- *Handbook for Decision-Makers: Land-Use Planning Recommendations—Adaptation Strategies for a Changing Climate in Ho Chi Minh City*
- *Urban Design Guidebook* as a tool for integrating climate change adaptation into planning and design decisions
- *Handbook for Green Housing* for disseminating good practices in urban design and architecture
- *Handbook for Community-Based Adaptation* as a guide for building resilient communities through local action

Contact

Project: Megacity research project TP. Ho Chi Minh
Michael Schmidt | Brandenburg University of Technology Cottbus–Senftenberg
Email: umweltplanung@tu-cottbus.de
Webpage: www.megacity-hcmc.org

Water Management in Lima (Peru)

Context

Lima, a desert city (9 mm annual precipitation), has a population of approximately 9.8 million and is growing at an annual rate of about 2%, largely due to the influx of poorer people from the provinces. This development puts additional pressure on informal settlements, which lack an appropriate supply of electricity, water, and sanitation. Consequently, the polarisation between rich and poor districts is increasing.

Water supply is mainly sourced from the Rímac River, which has an irregular flow due to the arid climate and due to significant seasonal rainfall variations in the Andean mountains. Furthermore, river flows from the Amazon catchment area are diverted in order to contribute to Lima's water supply while groundwater resources remain limited. The scarcity of water resources will further aggravate the situation, as Peru is the third most sensitive country to impacts of climate change on precipitation and water availability [Rosenberger, 2006]. This is likely to intensify even more in the future due to the El Niño phenomenon.

At present, the water supply network covers 80.6% of the population of Lima, whilst about 77% of the population are connected to the public sewer network. At present, only about 17% of wastewater receives some form of treatment. New plants are under construction; however, they will only offer a limited degree of wastewater treatment. The major quantity of wastewater is simply discharged into the rivers or directly into the Pacific Ocean. Furthermore, the potential for water reuse has not yet been fully exploited. The water sector strongly interconnects with the energy system, not only in the inherent need for energy for water and wastewater pumping and treatment, but even more so for the joint use of reservoirs for water supply and for energy production.

Objectives

The Lima Water Project (LiWa) aims to improve sustainable planning and management of the water and sanitation system in Lima through informed decision-making and stakeholder participation. The project draws particular attention to the impacts of climate change and to the promotion of energy efficiency in water and sanitation systems. More specifically, the project intends to develop adequate and locally beneficial solutions for different problems and contexts that contribute to an overall favourable water-management concept.

Approach

The LiWa project focuses specifically on the development and application of fundamental procedures and tools for participatory decision-making, based on informed discussions. The project builds upon modelling and simulation of the entire water supply and sanitation system within the megacity system of Lima. Furthermore, the project integrates findings from global circulation models, regionalised to Peruvian river catchments. The project also develops and evaluates options for reorganising the water tariff system in order to meet economic, ecological, and social requirements. Additionally, urban planning aspects are considered by developing the ecological infrastructure strategy, which is based on the concepts of water-sensitive urban design. With this holistic project approach, key issues and challenges of climate-responsive and energy-efficient structures of water and wastewater management can be adequately addressed.

Hence, the following work packages are being addressed:

1. Integrated scenario development
2. Downscaling of climate models and water-balance modelling
3. Macro-modelling and simulation system

Awareness-raising campaign for water saving and waste recycling for kids in Lima [Lukas Born]

4. Participation and governance approach
5. Education and capacity building
6. Economic evaluation of water-pricing options
7. Integrated urban planning strategies and planning support

Solutions

- Simulator for macro-modelling of the urban water system for informed decision-making
- Simulation of Lima's future development, taking into account climate-change effects on the water system for long-term planning
- Round-table discussions as new forms of governance in the water sector
- Water-pricing options and improvement of tariff structure
- Integrated urban planning strategies and planning support
- E-Academy for education and capacity building

Contact

Project: Sustainable water and wastewater management in urban growth centres coping with climate change—concepts for Metropolitan Lima, Peru
Manfred Schütze | ifak e. V. Otto-von-Guericke-Universität Magdeburg
Email: manfred.schuetze@ifak.eu
Webpage: www.lima-water.de

ADDIS ABABA: The Pilot Biogas Plant at the Institute of Technology is used as means of capacity development [Lukas Born]

Authors

Veena Aggarwal is a qualified economist who specialises in regulatory issues of the energy sector. Currently, she is employed as a fellow at The Energy and Resources Institute (TERI) and manages the Centre for Resources and Environmental Governance at the institute. Aggarwal's research focuses on regulation, tariff setting, and competition in the energy sector, as well as other issues concerning resource governance and sustainable development.

The Energy and Resources Institute |
veenaa@teri.res.in

Mamidi Bharath Bhushan is director of Centre for Action Research and People's Development, Hyderabad. He has been involved with civil society for more than twenty years in the areas of policy research, social safeguards, community development, education, food security, and governance. Bhushan's research interests include conflicts over natural resources, food systems, resettlement and rehabilitation, and tribal culture in India.

Centre for Action Research and People's Development | mbbhushan@gmail.com

Anne Dahmen worked as a junior research fellow at the Universität Göttingen and coordinated the pilot project Sustainable Street Food. She studied Geographical Development Research, Sociology and Cultural Anthropology at the University of Bonn and Cologne. In 2013, Dahmen joined adelphi Research.

adelphi Research GmbH, Berlin |
dahmen@adelphi.de

Haimanot Desalegne has a MA degree in Management and a post-graduate diploma in Communication. During the past two decades, he has been engaged in the development and implementation of different development programmes and projects in the NGO sector. Since 2009, he has been responsible for managing and coordinating waste management and other projects of Environmental Development Action (ENDA)-Ethiopia including the IGNIS project. Desalegne is country coordinator of ENDA-Ethiopia.

ENDA-Ethiopia, Addis Ababa |
haimanotd@gmail.com

Christoph Dittrich is professor and head of the Department of Human Geography at the University of Göttingen. His research focuses on land-use transformation in rural Southeast Asia and on urban food systems in South Asia. Dittrich is an advisory board member appointed by the German Government for Indo-German Cooperation (Indo-German Consultative Group).

Göttingen University |
christoph.dittrich@geo.uni-goettingen.de

Bernd Franke is a graduate of the University of Heidelberg and has more than thirty-five years of professional experience in environmental assessment projects in Europe, the USA, and Asia. He is a co-founder of the Institute for Energy and Environmental Research (IFEU) in Heidelberg, where he holds the position of scientific director. He is currently IFEU's project director for the BMBF-funded, RECAST Urumqi project, which focuses on how to improve energy efficiency in the building sector and in industry in the capital of Xinjiang, PR China.

Ifeu, Institute for Energy and Environmental Research, Heidelberg |
bernd.franke@ifeu.de

Magdalena Gack is a graduate student in the Masters programme, Integrated Natural Resource Management at Humboldt-Universität zu Berlin. She is a political scientist and worked as a research assistant in the project, Energy and Water of the Sustainable Hyderabad project (BMBF Megacity-Programme).

Humboldt-Universität zu Berlin |
magdalena.gack@gmail.com

Mekuria Gebru has a BSC degree in Applied Chemistry from Hawassa University and a MSC degree in Environmental Science from Addis Ababa University. Since 2011, he has been responsible for coordinating the pilot projects of IGNIS at Environmental Development Action (ENDA)-Ethiopia. Gebru is a senior project officer in ENDA-Ethiopia for the IGNIS project.

ENDA-Ethiopia, Addis Ababa |
mkrgbr@gmail.com

Frank Helten is a social scientist and has a PhD in philosophy from the Technische Universität Berlin (TUB). He began his career as an urban sociologist in Düsseldorf and in Algiers, where he joined an international study group. Helten was lecturer and scientist at Freie Universität Berlin, Gesamthochschule Kassel, and TUB. Currently, he works as an independent author and scientist. He has a wealth of experience in various social research fields and has coordinated several research projects for the Berlin Institute of Research (BIS) and has reviewed different research programmes for the European Commission.

Independent author and scientist |
Frank.Helten@t-online.de

Christian Hennecke studied architecture in Darmstadt and Tokyo. He worked for four years in Beijing at the China Architecture Design and Research Group (former design department of the Chinese Ministry of Construction). Hennecke is the general manager of Culturebridge Architects, an architectural design studio active in Rhine-Neckar region and China that he established in 2009. Since 2007, he has supported the RECAST Urumqi project in the fields of sustainable urban development and energy-efficient architecture.

Culturebridge Architects, Grünstadt |
chennecke@culturebridge-architects.com

Berthold Kaufmann, is a physicist by training, with a PhD degree. He is a senior research scientist at the Passive House Institute, which he joined in 2000. Kaufmann specialises in energy balance calculations (simulation) of buildings as a whole and on thermal properties of building façade components, especially thermal flux for design purposes. He consults and develops the design of highly insulated windows and heat pump systems, supporting architects and contractors on Passive House design for both new-builds and retrofits, including performing economic and financial analyses.

Passive House Institute |
berthold.kaufmann@passiv.de

Christian Kimmich is an agricultural economist and researcher at the Division of Resource Economics at the Humboldt-Universität zu Berlin. He has worked on the regional governance of energetic biomass utilisation, food-versus-fuel conflicts, as well as broader issues of ecological macroeconomics. Within the BMBF-funded Emerging Megacity Programme, Kimmich has conducted his PhD research on the sustainable provision of electricity for irrigation in agriculture from the perspective of evolutionary and institutional economics.

Humboldt-Universität zu Berlin |
christian.kimmich@hu-berlin.de

Michael Knoll was educated as an Industrial Management Assistant (*Industriekaufmann*), and has several years of experience in industry. Knoll studied Political Science at Frankfurt/Main and Berlin. Since 1989, he has been a researcher and co-ordinator of the Energy, Climate Protection and Air Pollution Control Unit at IZT—Institute for Futures Studies and Technology Assessment, Berlin. Knoll has extensive experience in the fields of energy and transformation processes, as well as technology assessment, futures studies, and evaluation.

Institute for Futures Studies and Technology
Assessment | m.knoll@izt.de

Ines Langer works as a research associate at the Institute of Meteorology, Department of Earth Sciences, at the Freie Universität Berlin. She has taught at the Institute since 1996 and is responsible for research activities in the field for microclimate measurements. Langer's research focuses on urban microclimates and the evaluation of climate models. For the Young Cities Project, she has simulated the microclimate of the 35-hectare area and projected the future climate up to the year 2100.

Freie Universität Berlin |
ines.langer@met.fu-berlin.de

Ming Liu graduated from the Northwest Architecture and Engineering Institute in 1985. He is been engaged in HVAC system design and research for twenty-five years. His research covers the seasonal energy efficient air-conditioning technologies in arid regions and the practical application of innovative designs. Liu contributed to the RECAST Urumqi project in the area of the energy efficient design of buildings.

Xinjiang Architectural Design and Research Institute, Urumqi | lium812003@gmail.com

Bernd Mahrin is a vocational training pedagogue and has a mechanical engineering degree. As assistant researcher at the Department of Vocational Education of the Technische Universität Berlin, he was responsible for vocational training in the Megacities Project, Young Cities | Developing Energy-Efficient Urban Fabric in the Tehran-Karaj Region. Furthermore, Mahrin works as a freelance consultant for the German Federal Institute for Vocational Education and Training (BIBB), for the Federal Office of Economics and Export Control (BAFA), and for several vocational training centres.

Technische Universität Berlin | bernd.mahrin@tu-berlin.de

Artur Mennerich is professor at the Ostfalia Hochschule für angewandte Wissenschaften Suderburg, Germany and Head of the Department of Sanitary Engineering. He acquired his PhD at the Technische Universität Braunschweig in Germany. Mennerich is a member of the International Water Association (IWA) and head of the Lower Saxony branch of the German Water Association (DWA). His research focuses on the management of wastewater and sewage sludge, nutrient removal, operation and energetic optimisation of systems for wastewater and landfill leachate treatment.

University of Applied Sciences Suderburg | a.mennerich@ostfalia.de

Lutz Meyer-Ohlendorf is a research associate at the Potsdam Institute for Climate Impact Research (PIK) in the BMBF-funded project, Sustainable Hyderabad. He has a Masters degree in Social Geography, Cultural Anthropology and Indology from Cologne University, whilst his PhD research focuses on developing a lifestyle typology of private households, explaining environmental consciousness and consumption behaviour, and revealing levels of lifestyle-induced GHG emissions. Meyer-Ohlendorf has developed the concept and coordinated the pilot project, Education for Sustainable Lifestyle (ESL) in Hyderabad, India.

Potsdam Institute for Climate Impact Research | meyer-ohlendorf@pik-potsdam.de

Bibhu Prasad Nayak has a PhD and is working as a research fellow at The Energy and Resources Institute (TERI), New Delhi. He studied natural resource economics and has worked in institutions and on collective action for participatory forest management in India for his PhD research. His research interest includes community-based natural resource management and the application of new institutional economics' tools for the analysis of environmental and natural resource governance issues.

The Energy and Resources Institute | bibhu.nayak@teri.res.in

Eva Nemcova is a researcher at the Institute of Landscape Planning and Ecology at Stuttgart University. She studied at the University of Brno, Czech Republic and obtained her diploma degree in Landscape Planning and Design at the University of Hanover, Germany where she received the Alfred Töpfer Foundation Scholarship. Nemcova previously worked at the landscape architecture offices Station C23 architecture landscape urbanism, Leipzig, at Stoss Landscape Urbanism, Boston and at osp urbanelandschaften, Hamburg on integrated landscape planning and design projects. She is a member of STUDIO URBANE LANDSCHAFTEN. Since 2011, she has been conducting research on open space planning and design in Metropolitan Lima within the LiWa project.

Stuttgart University | eva.nemcova@ilpoe.uni-stuttgart.de

Xiaoyan Peng has degrees in Landscape Architecture, Chinese, and Law from various universities. She heads the policies for energy-efficient design of buildings, developing renewable energy supplies, and science and technology management at the

Science and Technology Department of the Urumqi Construction Committee.

Science and Technology Department of Urumqi Construction Committee |pxiaoyan@163.com

Rossana Poblet holds a double Master's degree in International Cooperation and Urban Development from the Technische Universität Darmstadt, Germany and Universidad Internacional de Catalunya, Barcelona, Spain. She is employed at the Institute for Landscape Planning and Ecology at the Faculty of Architecture and Urban Planning at the University of Stuttgart developing the Lima Ecological Infrastructure Strategy with the LiWa Project. Poblet is a senior expert in urban development, landscape planning, informal settlements, and social housing. She has international experience in Peru, South Africa, Kosovo, and Germany.

Stuttgart University | rossana.poblet@ilpoe.uni-stuttgart.de

Nadia Poor Rahim obtained a Bachelor's Degree in Architecture at the Art University of Isfahan and has a degree (Dipl.-Ing.) from the Technische Universität Berlin (TUB). In 2010, she began a Masters course in Real Estate Management at the TUB. Poor Rahim worked as student assistant in the Megacities Project, Young Cities | Developing Energy-Efficient Urban Fabric in the Tehran-Karaj Region at the Department of Vocational Education of the Technische Universität Berlin. She recently started her career as assistant researcher in BMBF-funded lighthouse project, Mobile Learning Container.

Technische Universität Berlin | nadia.poorrahim@tu-berlin.de

Gisela Prystav is a qualified environmental engineer. She is scientific staff member of the Cooperation and Consulting for Environmental Questions (ZEWK/kubus), the TU Berlin's science shop for socio-ecological concerns. Her main focus is on inter- and transdisciplinary cooperation, sustainable water management, urban agriculture, and environmental protection in small and medium-sized enterprises (SME). In the UAC project kubus, Prystav was responsible for governance and capacity development and the pilot project UA and informal settlement.

Technische Universität Berlin, ZEWK/kubus | gisela.prystav@tu-berlin.de

Fritz Reusswig is a senior researcher at the Potsdam Institute for Climate Impact Research (PIK) and deputy head of the Domain Transdisciplinary Concepts and Methods. He has a Master's degree in Sociology, a PhD in philosophy, and a postdoctoral lecture qualification in sociology. Reusswig's major research areas are consumption, lifestyles, urban development, and climate change. He led climate change studies for Potsdam and Berlin. In the Sustainable Hyderabad project, he was responsible for the theme, "sustainable lifestyle", as well as the training for the Education for Sustainable Lifestyle pilot project.

Potsdam Institute for Climate Impact Research | fritz@pik-potsdam.de

Johannes Rupp has a degree in Forestry Science from the Universität Freiburg and a MSc. in Integrated Natural Resource Management from the Humboldt-Universität zu Berlin. Rupp's research comprises local and regional energy and climate-protection concepts on a national and an international level, including acceptance and participation. In the EnerKey project, he worked on stakeholder integration and socio-economic drivers at the Institute for Futures Studies and Technology Assessment (IZT), Berlin. Since 2013, Rupp has been employed at the Institute for Ecological Economy Research (IOEW) in Berlin.

Institute for Ecological Economy Research | johannes.rupp@ioew.de

Julian Sagebiel is an economist, currently employed at the Institute for Ecological Economy Research, Berlin. From 2009 to 2013, he worked at the Division of Cooperative Sciences at Humboldt-Universität zu Berlin, where he coordinated a pilot project on improving agricultural electricity provision in India within the BMBF-funded emerging megacity programme. He conducts his PhD research on consumer preferences in the electricity sector, focusing on India and Germany.

Humboldt-Universität zu Berlin | julian.sagebiel@hu-berlin.de

Karen Schmidt has a degree (Dipl.-Ing.) in Civil Engineering from the Brandenburgische Technische Universität Cottbus-Senftenberg, Germany. Since 2005, she has been employed at the Vocational Training Institute of Construction Industry association of Berlin-Brandenburg. Schmidt works as a project manager in national, international, and European building projects in the fields of sustainable and energy-efficient construction.

Vocational Training Institute of Construction Industry Association of Berlin-Brandenburg | k.schmidt@bfw-bb.de

Andrea Schultheis has a degree in Geography (Dipl.-Geogr.) from Universität Stuttgart. Since 2005, she is working with AT-Verband mostly in international BMBF research and development projects. She has worked in capacity-building, waste management projects and practical on-site training programmes for InWEnt in Zambia, Nigeria, Tanzania, and Uganda. Schultheis is a member of the board of AT-Verband and is project manager in the BMBF-funded IGNIS project.

AT Verband, Stuttgart | andrea.schultheis@at-verband.de

Dieter Steinbach has a degree in Geography (Dipl.-Geogr.) from Universität Stuttgart. His work activities have led him from intra-European projects for the EU Commission and BMBF, to Turkey, Egypt, Vietnam, and Sub-Saharan Africa during the past two decades. In the African context, Steinbach was especially involved in the education and training of local waste managers in theory and practice for GIZ/BMZ. Since 2005, he has been working with AT-Verband and, since 2011 he has been Chairman of the association. Steinbach is the coordinator of the BMBF-funded IGNIS project.

AT Verband, Stuttgart | dieter.steinbach@at-verband.de

Antje Stokman is Professor and Director of the Landscape Planning and Ecology at Stuttgart University. She participated in many international projects and was Associate Professor at Hannover University. Stokman's work focuses on strategies to develop infrastructure and ecological systems as a basis for sustainable urban form and the design of urban landscapes. She was awarded the Topos Landscape Award and the Lower Saxony Science Prize and is a member of the German National Advisory Council on Spatial Planning and of the Sustainability Council of Baden-Württemberg province.

Stuttgart University | antje.stokman@ilpoe.uni-stuttgart.de

Michael Waibel has a PhD in Human Geography. He is senior researcher at the Department of Geography at Hamburg University. Within the BMBF Megacity Ho Chi Minh project, Waibel was coordinator of the work package "Climate-Adapted Housing and Energy-Efficient Buildings". He worked as consultant for the University of Architecture in Ho Chi Minh City between 2007 and 2009. Waibel has published extensively on urban issues. He is co-publisher of the *Handbook for Green Housing*, sole publisher of the *Handbook for Green Products*, and editor-in-chief of the scientific journal *PACIFIC GEOGRAPHIES* and of the book series *PAZIFIK FORUM*.

Hamburg University | waibel_michael@yahoo.de

Christine Werthmann is an economist working as a PostDoc at the Division of Resource Economics at the Department of Agricultural Economics, Humboldt-Universität zu Berlin. After her studies in Marburg, Stellenbosch, and Berlin, she conducted her PhD research at the Philipps University of Marburg, investigating natural resource management in the Mekong Delta from an institutional perspective. Between 2010 and 2013, she led the Workpackages Energy and Water in the Sustainable Hyderabad project (BMBF Megacity Programme).

Humboldt-Universität zu Berlin | christine.werthmann@agrar.hu-berlin.de

Editors of the publications series:
Elke Pahl-Weber, Bernd Kochendörfer,
Lukas Born, Jan Müller and Ulrike Assmann

Editor of this volume:
Bernd Mahrin

Copy-editing: Anna Roos, Bern; Inez Templeton,
Berlin
Design and setting: Tom Unverzagt, Leipzig
Lithography: Bild1Druck, Berlin
Printing and binding: GRASPO CZ, a.s., Zlín

Bibliographic information published by the
Deutsche Nationalbibliothek

The Deutsche Nationalbibliothek lists this publication in the Deutsche Nationalbibliografie;
detailed bibliographic data are available on the
Internet at http://dnb.d-nb.de

jovis Verlag GmbH
Kurfürstenstraße 15/16
10785 Berlin

www.jovis.de

jovis books are available worldwide in selected bookstores. Please contact your nearest
bookseller or visit www.jovis.de for information
concerning your local distribution.

ISBN 978-3-86859-275-7